AMERICAN AUTHORS AND CRITICS SERIES

Published by Barnes & Noble under the General Editorship of FOSTER PROVOST *and* JOHN MAHONEY *of Duquesne University with the sponsorship of that University.*

ABOUT THE AUTHOR

RICHARD WALSER, former Guggenheim Fellow and Professor of English at North Carolina State College, edited *The Enigma of Thomas Wolfe: Biographical and Critical Selections*. An anthologist and biographer, he has published articles in *American Literature, Modern Language Notes, American Speech*, and other periodicals.

Thomas Wolfe, January 3, 1936   *Pack Library*

THOMAS WOLFE

An Introduction and Interpretation

RICHARD WALSER

Barnes & Noble, Inc.   New York

Publishers   Booksellers   Since 1873

To HARPER & BROTHERS, appreciation is expressed to quote from the following books by Thomas Wolfe: *The Web and the Rock,* copyright 1939; *You Can't Go Home Again,* copyright 1940; *The Hills Beyond,* copyright 1941; and *Mannerhouse,* copyright 1948.

Acknowledgement is also made to quote from: *The American Novel and Its Tradition* by Richard Chase, copyright 1957 by Richard Chase, reprinted by permission of Doubleday and Company, Inc.; *Letters of Maxwell Anderson,* edited by Howard Mumford Jones, Little, Brown & Company; and *The Selected Letters of Thomas Wolfe,* edited by Elizabeth Nowell, William Heinemann Ltd.

A number of quotations in this book are reprinted with the permission of Charles Scribner's Sons from *The Letters of Thomas Wolfe* by Elizabeth Nowell, copyright © 1956 Edward C. Aswell. Grateful acknowledgement is made for permission to reprint quotations from the following books by Thomas Wolfe: *Look Homeward, Angel,* copyright 1929 by Charles Scribner's Sons, renewal copyright © 1957 Edward C. Aswell, as Administrator, C.T.A. of the Estate of Thomas Wolfe, and/or Fred W. Wolfe; *Of Time and the River,* copyright 1935 Charles Scribner's Sons; *From Death to Morning,* copyright 1935 Charles Scribner's Sons; *The Story of a Novel,* copyright 1936 Charles Scribner's Sons; and *Thomas Wolfe's Letters to his Mother,* copyright 1943 Charles Scribner's Sons. Also, from *The Marble Man's Wife,* by Hayden Norwood, copyright 1947 Charles Scribner's Sons, and *Editor to Author: The Letters of Maxwell E. Perkins,* copyright 1950 Charles Scribner's Sons.

Photographs are from the Thomas Wolfe Collection, Pack Memorial Public Library, Asheville, N.C., and from the Thomas Wolfe Collection, Library of the University of North Carolina, Chapel Hill, N.C.

CONTENTS

ILLUSTRATIONS

CHRONOLOGY

1900   Thomas Clayton Wolfe born October 3 at Asheville, a resort town in the Blue Ridge Mountains of North Carolina, son of a tombstone cutter from Pennsylvania. His mother was a native of the mountain area.

1904   Accompanied his mother at the St. Louis Exposition.

1905   Entered Orange Street Public School in Asheville.

1908   Moved with his mother to The Old Kentucky Home at 48 Spruce Street, which she had purchased two years before.

1912   Began four years at the North State Fitting School, a private institution operated by Mr. and Mrs. J. M. Roberts.

1916   Entered the University of North Carolina.

1917   Summer romance with Clara Paul. In November his first published writing, a poem, appeared in the university magazine.

1918   Worked at Langley Field, Virginia, in the summer. October 19 his favorite brother, Benjamin Harrison, died during the influenza epidemic.

1920   Graduated from the University at Chapel Hill and entered Harvard.

1922   Received an M. A. in English from Harvard. His father, William Oliver Wolfe, died June 20.

1923   Completed an extra year at Harvard, studying playwriting under Professor George P. Baker. Had no luck selling his plays to New York producers.

1924   Accepted an instructorship in English at New York University in January. In October sailed for Europe. On New Year's Eve, encountered his friend Kenneth Raisbeck in Paris.

1925   Traveled in Europe. On September 10, aboard ship returning to America, met Mrs. Aline Bernstein. Resumed teaching at New York University. Still found no producers for his plays.

1926   Second voyage to Europe began in June. During July, in England, began a novel tentatively called "The Building of a Wall."

1927   In January was back in New York; devoted his entire time to the novel instead of returning to teaching. Lived in an apartment in Greenwich Village, rented for him by Mrs. Bernstein. Completed the first draft of the novel and sailed for Europe in July. Taught again at New York University in the fall.

1928   After several publishers rejected his novel, made a fourth trip to Europe in July. Attended "Oktoberfest" in Munich. "O Lost" accepted by Maxwell Perkins at Scribners.

1929   Returned to New York in January and taught part-time at the university. October 18 *Look Homeward, Angel* published, with violent reaction in Asheville.

1930   Finally gave up teaching in January, and at the same time made a break in his relations with Aline Bernstein. Sailed for Europe in May, after receiving a Guggenheim Fellowship.

1931   Returned to America and moved to Brooklyn to write.

1933   Completed draft of *Of Time and the River*.

1934   Worked with Maxwell Perkins on *Of Time and the River*.

1935   Went to Europe just before publication of *Of Time and the River* on March 8. Returned to New York on July 4. Settled in New York—now famous and successful. First trip to West Coast. *From Death to Morning* published November 14.

1936   Trip to New Orleans and Raleigh in March. *The Story of a Novel* published April 21. On seventh and last European trip, attended Olympic Games. Quarreled with Maxwell Perkins.

1937   In May, made first visit to Asheville since *Look Homeward, Angel*. Spent the summer at a nearby mountain cottage. Then lived in semiseclusion at a New York hotel. In December, signed a contract with Harpers.

1938   Worked strenuously on new fiction. In May, spoke at Purdue University and continued on to the Far West to tour national parks. In July, hospitalized in Seattle. After two operations at Johns Hopkins Hospital, died in Baltimore on September 15. Buried in family plot at Asheville.

1939   *The Web and the Rock* published June 22.

1940   *You Can't Go Home Again* published September 18.

1941   *The Hills Beyond* published October 15.

1945   Julia Westall Wolfe, Wolfe's mother, died December 7.

So, THEN, to every man his chance—to every man regardless of his birth, his shining, golden opportunity—to every man the right to live, to work, to be himself, and to become whatever thing his manhood and his vision can combine to make him—this, seeker, is the promise of America.

—You Can't Go Home Again

❧ ☙

He was a poet, the flung spear of their immortal life, and he sang the songs of all the poets that had ever sung and died. He was a poet, and upon his tongue there rolled the swelling tide of song of all the poets that had ever sung and lived. He was a poet, and he was the brother and the son, and the undying tongue, of all the poets that had ever sung and lived and died since time began. He was a poet, and the son of poets dead and gone, and a mighty poet in his own domain, and in his wild, unuttered blood there sang that night the wild, unuttered tongues of darkness and America. He was a poet, and all of the wild, unuttered tongues that he must sing were singing in his blood that night. And he stood here on the lid of night, upon this shore of the immortal dark, upon the undiscovered edge of all the brave new world of this America; and knew that still the tide was coming in upon the full, and that even yet, the Muses yet, had not yet reached their prime.

—The Web and the Rock

1

ᴥᔑ AMERICA AND POETRY

From the explorers on, the secret of America—that vast continent lost for centuries in deep tangled forests and slow spacious rivers—occupied the thinking of writers. Yet not till Walt Whitman came along did its mystery and fascination evoke a poetry and form equal to its riddle. In his last days, old Walt Whitman looked about him at the land which had disturbed his imagination for so long, and wrote that America was

> Perennial with the Earth, with Freedom, Law and Love,
> A grand, sane, towering, seated Mother,
> Chair'd in the adamant of Time.

Whitman died in 1892, and eight years later Thomas Wolfe was born.

Wolfe was no copy of Whitman. The ages in which they wrote saw to that. At one time, Wolfe even denied that he had read Whitman. But there were similarities: the raw, exulting, wild poetry of Whitman was echoed in Wolfe's gushing, unconventional, chaotic prose. And they were both enamored of a country which teemed with a beauty of life so bounteous that a man might have his head turned by the sheer abundance of it all. They lived and they died, often misunderstood by those whom they were most avid to reach, but without having lost the passion which animated them.

America was big in 1848 when Whitman twisted his way across the mountains and down the great rivers to New Orleans. It was big in 1904 when Julia Elizabeth Wolfe took her toddling fifth son from a state on the Eastern seaboard to the St. Louis Exposition far inland. Though their first long journeys occurred when one was twenty-eight and the other only three, neither of them ever forgot his first sight of America.

The poetry of America and its meaning, whether in Whitman's reckless free verse or in Wolfe's frenzied paragraphs, has nowhere else been more triumphant. And he who reads either of them must perforce be caught up in an optimism which is part patriotism and part philosophic radiance.

That is not the full story, of course. Both Whitman and Wolfe, being men and not angels, had their moments of dejection and betrayal. These moments came when sober reflection got the upper hand of blind love. But in the beginning and at the end, it was belief and affirmation which characterized them; it was America which symbolized a breadth and freedom sought by men everywhere; it was America which led to the good days. The two stand, with a handful of others like Hart Crane and Carl Sandburg, as those who found in their country a vision of life.

≈§ §≈

On the first page of his first novel, Thomas Wolfe wrote: "Each of us is all the sums he has not counted: subtract us into nakedness and night again, and you shall see begin in Crete four thousand years ago the love that ended yesterday in Texas."

Clearly Wolfe was thinking of himself. One cannot be sure,

my own prison, but I shall get me some beauty, . . . I shall find my way out of it yet, though it take me twenty years more—alone."

"Alone?" said Eliza, with the old suspicion. "Where are you going?"

"Ah," he said, "you were not looking, were you? I've gone."

Wolfe's "going" gradually assumed a purposefulness more significant than mere flight from disdained environments and influence; it became a retreat into discovery of self, and from self into that which made up self—America. America had been surveyed, Wolfe said, but it had never been explored. To tell its shapes and colors, a new language had to be invented, a speech different from that of the statistician and the realist, a lyric tongue to express the interior spirit of a people and a continent. He was aware of Whitman's language, but clearly Whitman's way was not what he had in mind. Something else again was needed to catch the beauty, awe, spaciousness, and frightening loneliness of America.

Everywhere were insignia of the boundless land. There were the trains moving through the darkness, the sounds of the boats in the harbors, the vast rivers draining the mighty states, and the terrible endless skies. And there were the arrogant multi-peopled cities, and the little courthouse towns, and the men and women—fearing, hoping, hating, loving. All these things had to be told. They had to be told because no writers, with the exception of Whitman and Dos Passos, had made any attempt to deal with the expanse of America or to get at an understanding of the scope and proportions and capacious life of a land using the English tongue but un-European in its enormous and sequestered insularity. It was a land of paradoxes, of course, a land of poverty and bounty, of defeat and success, of unfruitfulness and raw fecundity, of downcast hopes and bright promise. Wolfe saw it as a land of sophisticated Bostonians and Southern colored folk from Old Catawba, of luscious Jewish women and destitute jobless drunks, of despi-

5

cable sycophants and strong-armed Paul Bunyans. It was a nation constantly on the move—the trains, always the trains, shooting across high trestles in the nighttime and curling around the hillsides, the whistles blowing a message to the solitary farmhouses beyond the valley.

It is movement, perhaps, which most characterizes Wolfe's novels. Automobiles, boats, and trains hurl Eugene-George on to new experience. The seductive woman smoothing her legs in an upper Pullman berth is image and part of the fantasy and wish fulfillment of America. "Through you," Wolfe wrote Aline Bernstein after his first voyage to Europe, "I slid back into America again."

On the move, somewhere, would be found the glorious dream, symbolized by that beautiful, enticing woman. She (the idea of America, the woman) would be security against all degradations and failures. In her were longing and love, and Wolfe poured into his books a return of that love, even when she had to bear up under his chastisement; for only through love and desire was fulfillment possible.

Wolfe found out that love of land was not inherent, that "the way to discover one's own country was to leave it; that the way to find America was to find it in one's heart, one's memory, and one's spirit, and in a foreign land." He perceived this truth on seven trips to Europe. It was then that, from sheer separation, he loved America most. Away from it, always he was drawn back by memory and some unexplained urge within.

Wolfe's exploration of America was an emotional voyage, undertaken not by listing and describing from hearsay and imagination the various aspects of a land too broad to be encompassed within the experience and life of one man. Often he chose the little, touching, unnoticed thing—"the sound of a milk wagon as it entered an American street just at the first gray of the morning"—sending off a stream of recollection into the past too tender for the rough jags of the unreal and made-up. A recollection such as this stirred the affections, not the intellect. It glowed and warmed him. In 1930 from London he wrote:

"My longing for America amounts to a constant ache." From its tangible substance, Wolfe was able to evoke the emotional personality of his country, bringing it out of memory with all its haunting beauty.

It was filtered through his own consciousness, and from it he drew his strength—his strength as an artist. For Wolfe found, eventually, that America was in himself. "He was not 'celebrating' America, as Whitman had done," writes Alfred Kazin; "he was trying to echo it in himself." From it he had need to draw his life, his art, and his speech. It was no easy discovery, no easy task; but by 1936 he was able to proclaim:

> I have at last discovered my own America, I believe I have found my language, I think I know my way. And I shall wreak out my vision of this life, this way, this world and this America, to the top of my bent, to the height of my ability, but with an unswerving devotion, integrity and purity of purpose that shall not be menaced, altered or weakened by any one.

Fortunately, the language to wreak out his vision was already at his disposal. For the straight narrative scenes he had the tried-and-true techniques of realistic fiction, valid and versatile enough to carry the burden of his intention. Infused with Wolfe's peculiar ironic commentary, it served well. Yet, for those pages where a more rhapsodic expression was indicated to unfold emotional themes, he turned to poetry. He did not use the word poetry. Instead he was often heard to say: "I'd rather be a poet than anything else in the world. God, what wouldn't I give to be one!" Seemingly he had not equated with poetry a personal emotionality to which he was even then giving expression. But whether he understood or not, in the spontaneous quality of his lyric passages there were imagery and rhythm and frequently even meter.

Who has seen fury riding in the mountains?
Who has known fury striding in the storm?

7

> Who has been mad with fury in his youth,
> given no rest or peace or certitude by fury,
> driven on across the earth by fury,
> until the great vine of the heart has broke,
> the sinews wrenched, the little tenement of bone,
> blood, marrow, brain, and feeling in which great fury
> raged, was twisted, wrung, depleted, worn out,
> and exhausted by the fury which it could not lose
> or put away? Who has known fury, how it came?

This paragraph from *Of Time and the River*, extracted ver-batim and rearranged only by the breaking up of sentences into lines, exhibits the melody and luxury of speech Wolfe permitted himself.

When America itself was the subject, he adopted a less stilted pattern and a more rigid vocabulary.

> *I will go up and down the country,*
> *and back and forth across the country*
> *on the great trains that thunder over America.*
> *I will go out West where States are square;*
> *Oh, I will go to Boise, and Helena and Albuquerque.*
> *I will go to Montana and the two Dakotas*
> *and the unknown places.*

The opulence of prose-poetry, even with Wolfe's alert ear for speech and words, had its drawback: it was not fashionable in a decade which paid tribute to the starker vogue of journal-istic Hemingwayese.

Still, heritage would not be denied. When he was a boy, he was "raised" on poetry. At home, Wolfe's father declaimed the famous passages from Shakespeare, and the two often conversed in measured phrases. From his mother the lad learned how to embellish a story with simile and metaphor. For all three, Southern rhetoric—the high sounding locutions, the delight of a series of four- and five-syllable adjectives—glittered and flourished. In school and college, Wolfe sat to the rhythm of the great English masters. He was captivated by the Cavalier and

8

Swinburnian schools, by Donne and Sir Thomas Browne and Milton, and later by James Joyce. There were, too, the resounding cadences of the Bible, rich and lavish.

If Wolfe made no claim to being a poet—and he assuredly did not—the effects of a tradition and the admirations of student days had nevertheless their impact on his prose. In poetry he satisfied his yearning for emotional release, his eagerness for music. "I almost never attend a concert or symphony," he wrote. "My real interest has been in poetry." So, in his novels, he opened the floodgates; and as he did it, like D. H. Lawrence and Henry Miller, he uplifted fiction to a plane where it shared an identity with poetry. As one thinks about the matter, it is not really so unusual that the poet's techniques and art should be adapted to prose fiction. Poetry is the most primitive of literatures. Since historically the novel is but an offshoot of traditional poetry, the writers of English fiction of the last four hundred years, in abjuring rhyme and meter, have not necessarily abjured the language and style of poetry. The only strange twist is that hard upon such writers as Theodore Dreiser and Sinclair Lewis there could have been a Thomas Wolfe at all, or further that he was impelled to fling his dithyrambic passages across the stretch of America. In his paeans to Time and America, his hymns to Death, Loneliness and Sleep, his salutes to trains and rivers, and his tributes to night, Wolfe swept past the lyric optimism of Whitman into an epic abundance. The picture was completely there, as it always has been in the best poetry.

Perhaps he was able to write in rhapsodic vein because he was willing to be neglectful of current trends and fashionable dicta. But the reason is more that he was young with a young man's vision. It has been said that Wolfe retained his adolescence until the end, that he never worked away from a boyhood with its ideals and hopes, that he kept the pain and poetry of youth even when, in the later novels, he tried to send them on their way. There is some truth in the observation. Poetry—the best lyric poetry—is concomitant with morning, and Wolfe

9

wrote out of the morning of his life. Disillusionments which eventually disturbed him were soon replaced by faith.

The prose poems introducing each of the four major novels return and ring and give emphasis to the stories to be told. In them and in the colors they create, one may observe Wolfe's essential quality.

◦§   §◦

Every age responds to, though it does not always recognize, the best talents living in it. That Wolfe has endured in an age which is scientific and nonpoetic, in an age which no longer reads epics and verse narratives, is due in measure, of course, to his ability and perceptiveness and originality. Response to him has continued in spite of an academic criticism which, in the years since the publication of *Look Homeward, Angel,* has not been overly generous toward his seemingly untamed splendors. Order and restraint, not exuberance, have been the keynotes.

Yet it is obvious, often, that literary criticism pays little mind to a man's hunger. The love and necessity for poetry persist. Prose literature, no matter how orderly its manufacture, will be thin and unsatisfying without it. There must be youthfulness and innocence and intoxication and ideals and beauty. Wolfe has them all. In a nonpoetic age, there is nevertheless a need for poetry. In a scientific age, a prose literature which gives poetry to us, even in our unawareness, is honored.

◦§   §◦

When Tom Wolfe was a student at Harvard, he wrote a letter to his preparatory-school teacher Margaret Roberts:

. . . And when the poets die, the death of the nation is assured.

Well, I have returned to all this at midnight. The fires of the hearth have burned to warm, grey cones of powder. There is a roaring in the wind to-night, the streets are driven

bare, and my "autumn leaves" are falling already upon the
roof in a dry, uncertain rain. . .

Seven years after this letter was written, book-buyers picked
up an unknown author's first effort called *Look Homeward,
Angel*. Not yet were the poets dead, and not yet would a nation
succumb.

2

Before Wolfe's books can be appreciatively read, one must have a reasonable acquaintance with his biography. This is not necessarily true in the case of most writers, whose private, factual lives are less closely reflected in their work than are those of, say, Dickens and Proust, to whom Wolfe bears a resemblance in this matter. Even Dickens and Proust observed autobiographical chronology less stringently than Wolfe.

To present his biography is not simple, for no single Thomas Wolfe ever existed. There were five facets of the man. Wolfe was the fabulous man compacted of all the legends; he was the Eugene-George semiautobiographical hero of the four novels; he was the many-charactered person his friends knew; he was the man he thought himself to be and so wrote himself down in his letters to correspondents; and finally he was the undiscoverable person underneath the other faces. To understand the last, one must range among the first four and even then prepare to find himself some distance away.

Not even the familiar legend can be discounted. Here was a man about six and a half feet tall, each day working fifteen hours and writing thousands of words. After midnight, at the moment of physical exhaustion, he lunged to the street, took a few drinks, and talked continuously to anyone who would listen. Up the next day, he gulped down tons of coffee, stood writing in his heavy ledgers atop a refrigerator, occasionally moved his 240 pounds up and down his apartment, waved his hands and smoothed his long hair, threw a filled-up ledger into a huge packing case conveniently placed in the center of the room to receive just such literary matter, and, a fresh ledger before him, continued his endless narrative. A month or two later, his editor telephoned him to bring in his novel, and Wolfe yelled for a truck to haul the packing cases off to the publisher's office. One report said the manuscript of *Look Homeward, Angel* weighed twenty-five pounds. Even the day before his death, legend has it, he ordered watermelons for all the hundreds of nurses at Johns Hopkins Hospital.

"I eat, talk, write and do everything too much," he said. About eating: "That is my big extravagance—my ravening gut." In such sentences did Wolfe contribute to the legend as it began to form at the time his first novel was published; the fantastic stories flattered his imagination and he enjoyed the picture of himself as the eccentric genius. Even consciously he seems to have helped construct the legend. Perhaps Wolfe, still young enough to play a Byronic role, began to *be* the Eugene Gant that he had created. The idea intrigues, whether it can be supported or not.

By its definition, legend is never entirely false, and most of the Wolfe legend is anchored in fact. He was indeed much taller than the average; for a while he wrote in ledgers, a refrigerator occasionally displacing the ordinary desk; and eyewitnesses reported a stack of manuscript eight feet high. Yet legend can be counted on to eliminate and exaggerate and twist, just as the Eugene-George hero is merely one side of the author, and in itself an exaggeration and a twisting. If the real person is undiscoverable, the only thing left to do is to cite the available data and rest the case.

The Wolfe story begins in 1851 on a farm near Gettysburg,

Pennsylvania, where William Oliver Wolfe, son of an English father and a Dutch mother, was born. As a boy during the Civil War, he watched from the roadside the Southern troops moving toward the great battle. Later, wanderlust in his veins, he went to Baltimore and for five years apprenticed himself to learn the trade of stonecutting. His apprenticeship days over, W. O. Wolfe (the W. O. Gant of *Look Homeward, Angel*) was invited south to the sleepy little North Carolina capital city of Raleigh, where stonecutters were needed in the construction of the newly authorized state penitentiary. When the structure was nearly completed, the young workman set up shop in the center of town and in 1873 married a local belle, Hattie J. Watson. Quickly the marriage between independent laborer and society girl ended in divorce, and it was not till six years later that he married again, this time to Cynthia C. Hill, a milliner nine years his senior. Shortly afterwards, the new Mrs. Wolfe moved west to Asheville, a mountain village lying in the cool valley of the French Broad River, its healthful climate just then beginning to attract vacation-seekers and those who were sick in body. After she had set up shop, her husband followed and established his own business just across from the pulsing fountain in the town square. There was something inside him that had never wanted to be a stonecutter; he would have preferred the stage with its bombast and declamation and poetry; yet for a while he was satisfied, for in the hamlet surrounded on all sides by the steep, impressive Blue Ridge mountains he sensed a beauty which was absent in the rolling lands of the Pennsylvania countryside or the Maryland city or the flat plains of eastern North Carolina, and which compensated for some aesthetic depth which life had left vacant.

East of Asheville, the Swannanoa River pushed its way through the hills to a meeting with the French Broad. Along its banks were many sturdy farmers of Scotch-Irish descent, noted for their common sense, their native wisdom, and a gift of storytelling perpetually enriched by incidents from their capacious memory. Among these families was the household of

Major Thomas Carey Westall and Martha (Penland) Westall
with their eleven children, the fourth of whom was named
Julia Elizabeth, born in 1860. Not only was Julia the possessor
of the keen intelligence of her tribe; she had further enhanced
her birthright by attending school and becoming a teacher in a
day when education was by no means expected of all. In spare
months she took on a line of books which she peddled in the
surrounding area, and on one of these trips she met the milliner
Mrs. Cynthia Wolfe. The acquaintance led to her calling on
the bookloving stonecutter to whom she was able to sell, though
he had never during his residence in the postwar South renounced his ardent allegiance to the Republican party, a book
vindicating the Southern cause.

When Cynthia died in February, 1884, the twice-married
W. O. wasted no time. The proprieties and decent delay were
observed, and then he laid siege to the attractive little mountain woman who was schoolteacher and bookseller and withal
a satisfactory choice. The two were married on January 14,
1885, and before the year was up W. O. was father to his first
child, a daughter Leslie. On the death of the child at nine
months, Julia Wolfe busied her mind away from deep distress
by inviting boarders to her table. Not always did the growing
resort town have sufficient accommodations for its ever increasing number of visitors, and the little house at 92 Woodfin Street,
which W. O. had built, stirred with the chatter of vacationers.

As the years passed, Julia Wolfe (the Eliza of *Look Home-
ward, Angel;* the Aunt Maw of *The Web and the Rock*) so
prided herself on her money-making abilities that the boarders
were not sent packing even when her other children came along:
Effie (the Daisy Gant of Wolfe's first novel), born in 1887;
Frank (Steve), 1888; Mabel (Helen), 1890; the twins, Grover
Cleveland and Benjamin Harrison (first names unchanged in
Look Homeward, Angel), 1892; Fred (Luke), 1894; and six
years later, Thomas Clayton Wolfe (Eugene; George), born
October 3, 1900.

By 1900, Asheville, with an official population of 14,694, was

15

a lively social and tourist center. The principal hotels were the Battery Park and the Manor House. Four miles to the south on the French Broad, the millionaire George W. Vanderbilt had erected Biltmore, the most spectacular mansion in America. In the town, handsome buildings and schools and homes had been and were being built. The property evaluation of the city was over $5,000,000. The public library had more than 3,000 volumes. A dignified courthouse faced the fountain on the square, across from W. O. Wolfe's stonecutting shop.

On Woodfin Street, boarders and children crowded the porch of the house where the fifty-year-old artisan lived. There was singing around the piano, there were frequent recitations of poetry, and there was talk, much talk, all the time. Julia Wolfe —energetic, earthy, fun-loving, and egocentric—presided over the ménage ; and William Oliver Wolfe—imaginative, assertive, restless, and sometimes glum—joined in the hullabaloo when he was in the mood. The confluence of spirits and tempers and vastly alive people shaped a child.

It would be easy to say that young Tom was precocious, for he was talking well at twelve months and doing some simple reading at the age of two. His mother, sensing that this was her last baby, kept him close to her, brushing his heavy brown curls and feeding him from her breast till he was three and a half. In April, 1904, she took him along with some of the other children to the World's Fair at St. Louis, where she ran a boarding establishment called the "Carolina House" at Fairmount and Academy streets. When twelve-year-old Grover died of typhoid fever on November 16, Julia bundled up her possessions and returned to Asheville. Now more than ever she became interested in the boy. "It was a sad time for Tom," she later said.

In September, 1905, when the boy was not quite five, he entered the first grade at the Orange Street School. A neighbor's son was prepared to enroll, and Tom wanted to accompany him. Though Julia was sure he would not stay, she did not reckon on his determination ; from the very beginning he was a good stu-

Wolfe and his mother, 1909   *University of North Carolina Library*

17

dent. In the afternoons when he came home to Woodfin Street,
she pulled him to her lap and twisted his curls in her fingers.
Not till he was eight could she be persuaded to cut the curls,
and then only because a growing boy could not prevent them
from becoming infested. Soon, like all the Wolfe boys, Tom
went to work as one of a number of street-venders of the *Satur-*
day Evening Post whom brother Fred had selling the magazines
for him. One week in May, 1909, Tom bested the group with
a sale of sixty-one copies.

Meanwhile, in one of her real-estate transactions, Julia Wolfe
paid $7,000 for a large rambling house at 48 Spruce Street, two
blocks from the Woodfin Street property. To it she gave the
name The Old Kentucky Home (Dixieland, the "bloody barn"),
and there she found space for roomers and boarders and all her
brood except Mabel, who stayed behind on Woodfin to take care
of her father. Though drably painted, it was close to the town
square, and its bay windows and broad porches gave it a comfortable appearance. In the decade that followed, its huge
dining room often accommodated fifty hearty eaters who de-
voured the fresh meat and vegetables from Julia's mountain
farm.

As home life was less than cozy in such an atmosphere, Tom
turned to whatever diversions presented themselves. When he
was eight, he took the train to visit his married sister Effie in
Anderson, South Carolina. At a whistle stop on the railway line,
the conductor called out "Gantt's Station." The boy remarked,
"What an odd name!" To those who have read his novels, it is
obvious that he never forgot it. Already he was storing away
all the materials he was to use in his books.

By now he was reading continually. After sampling the then-
popular Horatio Alger, he turned to more solid fare. Another
diversion, and never a chore, was Orange Street School. Frequently he was singled out for praise. He won a spelling match
because he was the only student who could spell *asafoetida*.
And then one evening his teacher, J. M. Roberts (John Dorsey
Leonard), carried home a boy-scrawled but somehow not-so-

routine composition and showed it to his wife (Margaret Leonard), who, lover of good writing and good literature that she was, saw something unusual and praised it. She was determined that Tom Wolfe should be a student in the private school she and her husband were preparing to inaugurate in the autumn of 1912.

The North State Fitting School, located on Buxton Hill in Asheville, was planned for the sons of wealth and society. If Tom's teachers had not pleaded so vigorously, the $100 yearly tuition would never have been found to finance him. But eventually it was, and there for the next four years he stayed. For two of the winters, while his mother was in Florida pursuing real estate, Tom boarded at the school. He was fast developing into adolescence. At Christmastime in 1914, though he put on his first long trousers, he was still more interested in books than in girls. Raw life he observed mainly on his newspaper route. Mrs. Roberts—the mother of his spirit, he called her—was his English teacher at the school. She led him into Shakespeare and the poets. She encouraged his writing. "In every paper he turns in," she said to her husband, "you can count on seeing one word, one phrase or one sentence that proves he is a genius." To Tom, she was no less flattering, yet there was stern caution. On a theme she wrote: "I will never correct another one of your papers if you will not observe the rules of paragraphing! Pegasus has to be controlled, even though it must be by one who has no wings."

In the spring of 1916 his graduation from the North State Fitting School coincided with the observance of the tercentenary of Shakespeare's death. His essay on the English dramatist won him a medal. That the years of private schooling had been worth while, his parents were proud to admit. Tom's record of college entrance credits represented solid study: geography 3, English 3, Latin 3, Greek 2, mathematics $2\frac{1}{2}$, and history 1. Obviously he was no ordinary preparatory-school graduate. Awkward, gangling, about six feet in height, with dark brown hair and brown eyes, a pair of enormous feet imbalanced by a small head—this strange lad, still fifteen years old, looked out on a world which seemed to have little relationship to the world of books he loved.

Like their father and mother, the Wolfe children were working folk, and though Tom's brother Fred had attended Georgia Tech intermittently, not till Tom's graduation was a liberal arts course in a university for one of them ever thought of. Of course, there was a difference now. As far as books went, Tom was unusual, so unusual that W. O. thought here was the chance to have a lawyer in the family—a lawyer, a politician, maybe a governor of the state. He agreed to pay the college fees and, in spite of Tom's wish to attend the University of Virginia, told him sharply, "You are a North Carolinian and you are going to patronize your own State."

In that fall of 1916, edging on his sixteenth birthday, the lanky, green freshman entered the University of North Carolina, hardly more than a good provincial college down the mountains over two hundred miles to the east in the agricultural part of the state. Along with the eleven hundred other students, he registered for his courses and settled down to a dull and, for him, unhappy autumn. The village of Chapel Hill provided not even the excitement of a growing town like Asheville. He was not enchanted. As he ambled along the gravel paths underneath the tall oaks on the campus, he was the butt of sophomoric pranksters who delighted in his unusual height. Not even his election as vice-president of the Freshman Debating Club brought him peace or satisfied his ego. Frequently he moved his living quarters from dormitory to private home and back again, and his grades that year in English, Latin, and Greek were only average. He sank to a "4" in mathematics!

The following summer he eagerly returned to Asheville, determined to get his father's permission to transfer to Princeton; but the old man had not lost his visions of a lawyer-son traditionally trained at the state university to occupy the Governor's Mansion in Raleigh. Furthermore, America had entered World War I, and capricious notions were not to be endured. Perhaps it was the time for it to happen, but that summer Tom Wolfe fell in love completely and desperately. The girl was Clara Paul (Laura James), up from eastern Carolina for a vacation at The Old Kentucky Home. The fact that she was five years his senior, that she was soon to be married, and that her young brother accompanied the lovers wherever they went, seems not to have dampened the ardor of the young suitor. When Clara departed to join her fiancé, the boy was disconsolate. On his way back to Chapel Hill, he visited his brother Ben in the tobacco city of Winston-Salem and re-entered college.

The War had depopulated the student body to a mere seven hundred, most of whom were student-soldiers—but not Wolfe, whom no uniform would have fitted even if he had been old enough to participate in the military program. The army was only another of life's rejections, and Tom Wolfe escaped to poetry, where he could be a hero in imagination. What apparently was his first published writing appeared in the *University of North Carolina Magazine* in November, 1917. Here is the second stanza of "A Field in Flanders":

> A war-ripped field,—with what a tale to tell!
> A tale to cause the souls of kings to quake,
> For here, within a smoking, bloody Hell,
> Ten million risk their lives for Freedom's sake.

While neither this ingenuous poem nor the gushing tribute "To France" a month later foreshadowed literary genius, Tom was so delighted to have these poems in print that he determined to go into journalism instead of into law. For the *Magazine* he carefully wrote a piddling short story titled "A Cullenden of Virginia," in which during an assault on the Western front a scion of brave Southern aristocrats overcame his cowardice to aid a wounded soldier.

The renown Tom received from these efforts—in an atmosphere where renown was easily won—raised his spirits. Suddenly he started joining everything: a social fraternity, the various campus publications, a literary club, the track team.

He wanted to improve his slovenly appearance. He wrote Ben to send him whatever discarded clothes were handy, for most of his own were quite "frayed." His grades improved: he made "I" in English and only in chemistry did he merely slide by.

In the summer of 1918 his poetic patriotism led him to the war-busy area of Norfolk. He was still not of an age to join the campus Student Army Training Corps, but he was not too young to "do his bit." For a while he was employed as a time-checker at Langley Field, later as a clerk on the government docks at Newport News. Several times he took the ferry to Portsmouth, where the now-married Clara Paul lived, and hovered a distance from her house in hopes he would see her.

Except for that spurt of activity in the previous spring, Wolfe's college days had been rather uneventful, his studies labored, and only his insatiable appetite for books bore any resemblance to life in the days of the North State Fitting School. But in the fall of 1918 he came under three teachers who were to have permanent influence. One was Edwin Greenlaw (Professor Randolph Ware in *The Web and the Rock*), professor of composition and scholar in Elizabethan literature. To Wolfe as to others in his classes—LeGette Blythe, Jonathan Daniels, Paul Green, to name but a few who were to become writers—he imparted a love of letters beyond anything they had known. A second was Horace Williams (Vergil Weldon in *Look Homeward, Angel;* Plato Grant in *You Can't Go Home Again*), a Hegelian philosopher who irritably shook his students into questioning the truth of all assertions. A third was Frederick H. Koch, bright-eyed professor from the Midwest who had just arrived in Chapel Hill to begin classes in playwriting. As Wolfe moved from lesson to lecture, the world expanded. He read, he wrote, he thought.

Then late in October, during the influenza epidemic, he was called home. His favorite brother Ben was ill. A few days afterwards, Ben died. This, Wolfe later wrote, affected him more than any other event in his life, and no one who has read *Look Homeward, Angel* will doubt it. Except for his mother, who seemed always to be escaping him, he now felt cast off and alone. He returned to the campus and, with an abandon bordering on delirium, threw himself wholeheartedly into its life. One moment he took himself quite seriously as of old, the next he handed himself over to the gag men and played up his comic figure and manner.

When called on to read his theme in Greenlaw's class, he jerked from his pocket (to the delight of all) a roll of toilet paper on which the words were written. Under Williams, he compensated for such tomfoolery by carrying off the Worth Prize for his essay "The Crisis in Industry." For Koch, he dashed off one-act plays of the mountain people around Asheville: "The Return of Buck Gavin," "The Third Night," "Payment Deferred," and one satirizing college elections, "Concerning Honest Bob." Several of them found their way into the *Magazine*.

His playwriting he took at least half-seriously. A fellow student in the Carolina Playmakers' class reported how "his great frame hunched forward, a nervous hand continually at his black [brown?] mane, his nostrils sniffing, like those of a charger eager to be off." Paul Green said that Wolfe, at this period a busy campus personality, always procrastinated in his assignments, then sat up all night writing pages to be presented at the appointed time, when he would come to class "hollow-eyed, shaggy-headed, unkempt and stuttering, and babble through the reading of his play."

When Tom wished, he could deliver a talk so ridiculously humorous that he was generally first choice among program-planners for the undergraduate smokers. During the following week he could act out his gloomy hero, Buck Gavin, on the Playmakers' stage. Tom Wolfe was popular and he was famous on the little knoll of Chapel Hill and for a while he was happy.

His last year at the university was glorious. Tapped for practically every honor except Phi Beta Kappa, he roamed the campus as a favorite. He journeyed to Richmond to witness his team's defeat of the University of Virginia in football. "The

Sweetest Story Ever Told," he headlined his account in the *Tar Heel,* the student newspaper which he edited. The report, it has been pointed out, was the first of his writing to indicate the style toward which he was tending. For the *Tar Baby,* a humorous magazine, he wrote an entire issue, lampooning a Raleigh morning newspaper. In the spring of 1920 the *Yackety Yack,* college annual, called him a "genius." And he was, too, not only to his fellow students, but also to his favored professors, though not always did the dons give him their top marks. Wolfe's courses and his grades during his junior and senior years reveal the contour of things to come:

1918–1919	Fall	Winter	Spring
Playwriting (Koch)	2	2	1
Advanced Prose Composition (Greenlaw)	-	1	1
Elizabethan Drama (Greenlaw)	2	2	2
Ethics, "a study of the forces that shape life" (Williams)	-	2	1
Military training	P	-	-

1919–1920	Fall	Winter	Spring
Journalism	2	1	1
Advanced Dramatic Composition (Koch)	2	2	2
Literature of the English Renaissance (Greenlaw)	2	2	-
Logic (Williams)	2	2	1
Modern European History (H. McG. Wagstaff)	-	-	2
English seminar	-	-	2

Julia Wolfe came down for his graduation. What would happen to him would be determined around the family council table at Asheville.

❧ ☙

When an offer came to teach at a military school near Asheville, the family urged Tom to accept, for his going to work

24

would put an end to the financial burden they all resented. Yet the graduate had no notion of pursuing the course of a schoolmaster; secretly he thought of himself as a playwright. To reveal such a fantasy would have outraged the practical Wolfe family; so the boy, in a businesslike way, gave the impression that he wished to take up journalism and announced his intention of going to Harvard; his real reason, however, was to study in the 47 Workshop of Professor George Pierce Baker, friend of Koch. "I'm going to Harvard if I have to borrow the money," he said. When W. O. made clear he would provide for no further education, Tom turned to his mother who agreed to pay the bills. (Between 1886 and 1921 the records show Mrs. Wolfe to have been party to forty-one real-estate transactions.)

In the fall of 1920, as he joined the other six thousand students at Cambridge, he passed into a new world. "The old democratic atmosphere of Chapel Hill is unknown here," he wrote his mother. To reduce the effect of the drastic difference in environment, he rented a room at 48 Buckingham Street, where Professor N. A. Walker of Chapel Hill was settled for the year. In the house were other Carolina students: Albert Coates, William Polk, and Skinner Mitchell.

That first autumn Wolfe's teachers included John Livingston Lowes, who read his manuscript of *The Road to Xanadu* to the class even while he was in the process of writing it. Wolfe was enthralled at Lowes' revelation of the working of Coleridge's memory and pondered "how retentive of all it reads is the mind and how, at almost any moment, that mass of material may be fused and resurrected in new and magic forms."

In Baker's class he was at first a bit taken back. Baker (Professor Hatcher in *Of Time and the River*) was an inspired teacher who somehow had managed to turn the seemingly impossible trick of transforming college students into successful Broadway playwrights, among them Eugene O'Neill, Philip Barry, Sidney Howard, and S. N. Behrman. While Wolfe wished to follow in their footsteps, he discovered that his Southern provincialism was in conflict with the aesthetic and intellectually snobbish members of the class, who were more archly "disturbed" that American society shunned its artists than they were busy writing plays in which the weaknesses of American institutions were exposed. In the company of such elevated conversationalists, Wolfe was shy; he rarely participated in the class round table.

Instead of switching to the precious concerns of his classmates, he began working over a drama called "The Mountains," more in line with the Koch folk-gospel. In it, a hill-born doctor, educated in the city, returned to his mountain region and became an unwilling participant in a feud. When produced by the Workshop in 1921, "The Mountains" failed with the audience but made such a favorable impression on Baker that Wolfe decided to expand it into three acts.

During his first year at Harvard, the gregarious nature he had developed in those last semesters at Chapel Hill subsided, and once again he turned to reading. The Widener Library became his refuge, and there he sated his appetite with volume after volume. One particular book must be mentioned. After reflecting on Walter Pater's *Marius the Epicurean,* he jotted down in his notebook Pater's idea of building a wall about oneself to shut out town, family, and society. The wall did not symbolize a withdrawal from life, but rather it protected one so that he could select the "fulness of life."

Before enrolling for the Harvard summer school in 1921, Wolfe left the Walker home and moved to 42 Kirkland Street —one of a series of migrations about Cambridge which was to last for the next two years. Though the Kirkland Street room was only four dollars a week, he found it hard that summer to pay the rent and still have enough money left over to fill his stomach. Back in Asheville, his family seemed to have forgotten him after his long absence from home, for his pleading letters were ignored. If it had not been for two eccentric old Cambridge ladies (portrayed as Miss Potter and Miss Flitcroft in *Of Time and the River*), he might have fared worse than he did. During these disconsolate days, he began to think of himself as "different" and expressed fears of appearing "highbrow" when he eventually returned to Asheville. Asheville was in his thoughts a good deal of the time. Scorning the Cambridge student dramatists with their praise of such writers "of debauched plays as Wycherley or Congreve" for their *"infinite* knowledge of life," he wrote his brother Frank that there was "a good play in Asheville. . . There's a play in everything that lives if we only had the power to extract it."

At the beginning of the second year as a graduate student in English, he was called to Baltimore where his father was ill with cancer at Johns Hopkins Hospital. A day after his return to Cambridge, the Workshop produced "The Mountains" at the Agassiz Theatre at Radcliffe, and when the audience found it "depressing," he buried himself more than ever in books. He changed rooms again—to 67 Hammond Street—and there his bare quarters resembled those he was to occupy the rest of his life. Manuscript, notebooks, and sections of plays lay scattered everywhere, and various publications, not texts but casual choices picked up in a moment of curiosity and only partially read, all but fell from the tables and chairs. He kept a notebook in which he recorded bits of wisdom. If he was guilty of such sophomoric enthusiasm as remarking on the "splendid serenity of Emerson" and writing that James M. Barrie was the greatest English-speaking dramatist in the world, he nevertheless put everything he read into the back of his mind. Forgetting was not a fault. Occasionally he thought about the future. "I have decided to devote my life to the drama, if I have any gift in that direction," he affirmed, then afterwards, with some sorrow asserted that "The conviction has grown on me that I shall never express myself dramatically." As is a young man's wont, he suffered indecision and inadequacy.

In the spring of 1922, after some difficulty completing a French requirement, he was awarded an M.A. degree. His grades were A's, excepting some B's under Baker and Lowes. Here is his Harvard record:

Playwriting (Baker)

The Forms of Drama, a survey from Greek times to the present (Baker)

The Poets of the English Romantic Period (Lowes)

Studies in the Literature of the Renaissance, continental and English to 1557 (Lowes)

The Drama in English from 1590 to 1642 (John Tucker Murray)

American Literature (Chester Noyes Greenough)

Philosophy: Esthetic Theory (Herbert Sidney Langfeld)

British History (Charles Howard McIlwain)

In these classes his reports and term papers were no hasty efforts. Generally they ran to seventy pages or so. In addition to the courses taken for credit, Wolfe audited George Lyman Kittredge's Shakespeare and Irving Babbitt's Literary Criticism of the Neo-Classic Period. No one can deny that, in both Chapel Hill and Cambridge, Wolfe had had some of the best teachers in America.

Following graduation, while he was considering an appointment to the English Department of Northwestern University, he was called home. His father, ill for the past eight years, died on June 20, 1922. During the summer Wolfe stayed in Asheville and finally, on the basis of an anticipated legacy from his father's estate, got his mother's permission to return to Harvard for a third year with the avowed purpose of reading, writing, and attending Baker's 47 Workshop course—nothing more.

His last year of university life—he lived at 21 Trowbridge Street—was a happy one. Finally had come a sense of acceptance, and there were many close friends, including Baker's chief assistant Kenneth Raisbeck (Francis Starwick). Though many plays were begun and few were completed, a drama with the working title of "Niggertown" stretched toward fulness. He thought constantly of his father—"the most unique human being I have ever known"—and wrote Julia Wolfe to "guard Papa's letters. . . . He is headed straight not for one of my plays, but for a series." Though he depended heavily upon Baker, he felt the restraints of supervision and wrote that admonitions to "balance, equipoise, or moderation" would cause him only to "burst forth the more intemperately at the end."

In May, 1923, his full-length play *Welcome To Our City,* an outgrowth of "Niggertown," was given by the Workshop. With its forty-four actors and four-hour production time, it was the first of his work to employ a familiar scene (Asheville, "Altamont") and characters he had known. In it Wolfe satirized the real-estate interests of a Southern town who tried to evict the Negroes from a central location in order to establish a white district there. When the Negroes resisted, racial tension developed. Yet the race issue was not paramount: Wolfe struck hard at the wrongs of dilettantism, prejudice, hypocrisy, and greed as he saw them, and so jammed his play with sharp episodes that he failed to provide it with adequate dramatic unity. But the audience, in spite of protests over the great length, was impressed, and Wolfe was ecstatic. He sat down and wrote his mother:

> I know this now: I am inevitable. I sincerely believe the only thing that can stop me now is insanity, disease, or death. The plays I am going to write may not be suited to the tender bellies of old maids, sweet young girls, or Baptist Ministers but they will be true and honest and courageous, and the rest doesn't matter. If my play goes on I want you to be prepared for execrations upon my head . . . God is *not* always in his Heaven, all is *not* always right with the world. It is not all bad, but it is not all good, it is not all ugly, but it is not all beautiful, it is life, life, life—the only thing that matters. It is savage, cruel, kind, noble, passionate, selfish, generous, stupid, ugly, beautiful, painful, joyous,— it is all these, and more, and it's all these I want to know and, by God, I shall, though they crucify me for it. I will go to the ends of the earth to find it, to understand it, I will know this country when I am through as I know the palm of my hand, and I will put it on paper, and make it true and beautiful.

Wolfe, about 1913   *University of North Carolina Library*

He stayed on in Cambridge after commencement, writing a play to which he would eventually give the name *Mannerhouse,* then with Baker's benediction left for New York to dispose of his work to professional producers. In September he lived at 439 West 123rd Street in the apartment of some old Chapel Hill friends. There was a brief visit to Asheville, and the rest of the autumn was spent waiting for the Theatre Guild's decision on *Welcome to Our City.* Lawrence Langner wanted him to cut it by thirty minutes, to eliminate two of its ten scenes, to reduce the number of characters, and to tighten the plot. For Wolfe, the job was impossible. Always his impulse was to expand, not contract. By the New Year he was discouraged with immediately becoming a successful playwright, his money was gone, he was "in rags," and he was looking for a job.

In January, 1924, he accepted an instructorship in English at the Washington Square College of New York University. For a sum of $1800, he was signed, February through August, to teach three courses in freshman composition. Near the college building, he rented Room 2220 at the Hotel Albert on 11th Street (Hotel Leopold in *Of Time and the River*), a family establishment where he worked out arrangements with the clerk to handle his checks and lend him money occasionally from his account. Meanwhile, he wrote his mother, he would have to continue on her "bounty" till the first pay came in March. Later he remarked on what "a poor economist" he was and how money had no value for him except to make him forget the fact that he ever wanted it.

At the school, from almost the first, Wolfe was a privileged person. The head of the English Department, Dr. Homer A. Watt, treated his new six-foot-four instructor with considerable understanding, allowing him favors denied his colleagues. Yet Wolfe was not entirely happy, and certainly he was unprepared for the type of students before him, so unlike those at Chapel Hill or Cambridge. Most were second-generation Americans from lower middle-class families, avid for knowledge, and uncomfortably persistent as they crowded near his desk at the

31

end of the hour with questions. Though begrudgingly, most of them began to like him, watching their giant of a teacher as he strode the classroom, reading or reciting poems excitedly, his perspiration flowing. Perhaps they dreaded his disfavor, for Teacher Wolfe gave very few A's and an unbearable number of F's. As the months passed, Wolfe found that the most disagreeable aspects of teaching concerned the endless themes which had to be read and graded. His "Presbyterian conscience" would not let him loose for entertainment or playwriting till every paper was marked.

Wolfe had welcomed the teaching position because he planned to use his free time for writing, but the enervating freshman themes drained his spirits for creativity. Not till the short Easter vacation did he pick up *Mannerhouse* again, and then he was happy, and the old beckoning of fame came back and he thought he would one day touch the far-off clouds. Soon he was shouting, "I am twenty-three, and a golden May is here. The feeling of immortality in youth is upon me. I am young, and I can never die." As the summer waned, he visited his wealthy artist friend Olin Dows (Joel Pierce) at Rhinebeck on the Hudson, next door to the Franklin D. Roosevelts with the Delanos and Astors nearby. He was waiting for autumn, and this time his plan would not fail.

Like his father, Thomas Wolfe had a yen to travel. So saving every cent possible, he made plans to go to Europe, his mother agreeing to come to his aid when his own cash was gone. To replace him at Washington Square came John S. Terry (Jerry Alsop), an old crony from Chapel Hill days. With all matters settled, a brief trip to Asheville prefaced the great hour on October 25, 1924, when Wolfe boarded the *Lancastria* in New York.

There was a month in England, and then he went on to Paris, where on his third day at a cheap hotel in the Latin Quarter something happened which dejected him more than anything "since the death of my brother Ben six years ago." His handbag, with the prologue and three acts of *Mannerhouse*, was stolen from the hotel entryway. As soon as he could adjust to the gloomy situation, he shut himself away and started re-creating the entire script. Then before it was completed, he met with Kenneth Raisbeck on New Year's Eve and embarked on those several weeks of comic grotesquerie rather faithfully described in *Of Time and the River*. There seems to be no doubt that Thomas Wolfe now fell in love for the second time. Hovering near Raisbeck were two mature, aristocratic Boston women, the younger of whom was apparently attracted to Raisbeck. Though five years older than Wolfe, she nevertheless acquired his instant affection. Obviously Raisbeck was incapable of emotional involvement with either. Before the weird foursome wore itself out, Wolfe wrote,

> I'm hopelessly, madly, desperately in love with a woman who doesn't care a tinker's damn about me. She's in love with someone who doesn't care a tinker's damn about her. To make it harder, I know him: he's one of my best friends.

When his finances would not allow a motor trip to the south of France with the three of them, he took off for Orléans to cool his ardor.

There he became acquainted with the Countess Constance Hillyer de Caen (La Comtesse de Caux in *Of Time and the River*, p. 830), who pounced upon him, boasting of her seventeen trips to America to renew her acquaintance with the American troopers whom she had befriended during the war. He wrote his mother:

> I met a real countess and spent the day at the magnificent chateau of a real marquise, both of whom had worked for the American soldiers, during the war, both of whom were pulling the leg of every American who could give them publicity. They laid themselves out for me, thinking I was a great American journalist, who would tell all the American papers about it.

In the spring he went on to Lyons, Avignon, Marseilles, and finally San Raphael, where he stayed for more than two months.

Though still "suffering from a bad attack of heartbreak," for a while he was consoled by a lonely mother and her daughter. In the summer there were shorter visits to Italy, to Switzerland, and a return to France and England; and in August, 1925, he sailed for home to resume his teaching at New York University.

✥ ✥

Aboard ship, he met the woman who was to be his constant companion for the next five years. Aline Bernstein (Esther Jack in *The Web and the Rock*), a Jew some eighteen years older than Wolfe, was married. Her husband's wealth did not deter her from an established career in the theatre as costumer and scene-designer. Evidently she was attracted to Wolfe partially because she understood his ambition to be a playwright. But whatever the cause, Wolfe was not himself unresponsive. He dashed to his desk at the college classroom building, exclaiming, "I'm in love! I'm in love!" By October he and Mrs. Bernstein were seeing each other daily; and it was evidently she who urged the Provincetown Theatre and the Theatre Guild to reconsider production of his plays.

The academic year 1925–26 passed exultantly, Mrs. Bernstein faithfully by him. With his salary raised to $2,000, he kept earnestly at his freshman and sophomore classes, entreating that he be spared the early morning hours; for, he said, he was "nightowlish." Once again, his hopes were high that his plays would be accepted. More and more he felt estranged from Asheville, for there, it seemed to him, his family and everyone else were insanely caught up in a sordid real-estate boom and madly grasping for wealth. Putting by what cash he could, he planned a second visit to Europe. On June 23 he sailed on the *Berengaria*. Then, without warning that he had ever contemplated a novel, he wrote from Bath, England, on July 19:

> I have begun work on a book, a novel, to which I may give the title of "The Building of a Wall"—perhaps not; but because I am a tall man, you know perhaps my fidelity to walls

and to secret places. All the passion of my heart and of my life I am pouring into this book—it will swarm with life, be peopled by a city, and if ever read, may seem in places terrible, brutal, Rabelaisian, bawdy.

Three years later this manuscript was published as *Look Homeward, Angel*. Apparently Wolfe started the book at Ilkley and, with the support of Mrs. Bernstein who had joined him, completed the outline there. By September he had two rooms in Chelsea, a quiet section of London where he was writing furiously. Later at Waterloo, he saw James Joyce but did not try to make his acquaintance. His news for homefolk was that the book was going great. During the autumn in England, and on the Continent as he went back and forth from country to country, the pages multiplied astoundingly. With his inventive brain abounding with the sights and smells of Asheville, there was no stopping. He felt more alone than ever. "I suppose in every family there's always a stranger, always an outsider. In our family Ben was the stranger until his death—I suppose I'm the other one," he wrote his mother.

Back in New York in January, 1927, Wolfe was persuaded by Mrs. Bernstein not to return to his teaching job but to stick to the novel. For $35 a month she rented a garret for him over a tailor's shop in a run-down building at 13 East 8th Street. He might repay her, she insisted, when he later got a job with an advertising firm she knew about. Though the shabby hide-away, without bath but with a pleasant skylight, was a dilapidated coldwater flat, the writing went well and rarely did he leave it except to go uptown to the Harvard Club for his mail and a shower. "I write from eleven o'clock at night till six in the morning," he proudly informed Olin Dows, "and get up at one or two o'clock. For the first time in my life, I'm seriously at work. It is mad, drunken, wild . . ."

Mrs. Bernstein wanted him to become associated with the prominent people in her artistic set; but his eyes were different from hers. At an elegant party, he was introduced to William

Rose Benét and Elinor Wylie (Rosalind Bailey in *The Web and the Rock*)—but "I hated them so that I managed to insult them all before the evening was over." Among the wealthy and distinguished, Wolfe was warmed only by the patient, unassuming Dows, who was genuinely solicitous about his work. During June, Wolfe spent a few weeks at the gatekeeper's lodge of Dows' Foxhollow Farm at Rhinebeck—"a little bit of heaven with a little river, a wooded glade, and the sound of water falling over the dam all through the night." It should have been an ideal spot for writing, but there were distractions in the form of evening dinners and a Fourth of July visit to Vincent Astor's estate with its miniature railroad. Soon, accompanied by Mrs. Bernstein, Wolfe was off on his third European tour, this time to France, Germany, Austria, and Czechoslovakia. The short trip was rather a respite to celebrate his having completed the manuscript draft of the novel.

In September, after more than a year's absence from the university, Wolfe resumed his classes. Mrs. Bernstein arranged an apartment for them at 263 West 11th Street, where she used the big front room as a studio and theatrical business office. Wolfe, living in the rear of the one floor, paid half the $135 monthly rent. There, almost every afternoon till the following March, he dictated from his ledgers the indecipherable pages of his novel to a student typist. A university friend who often visited him at this time said "the place was in incredible disorder, as Tom's homes usually were, with a minimum of furniture and with manuscripts and books and hundreds of 'Freshman themes' thrown everywhere."

Though freshman themes were still the terror of his life, now more than formerly he sympathized with the creative tortures of his students. He gloried that he had never added a grade to a paper without some sensible and encouraging comment. He never missed classes and regularly returned the corrected themes, sometimes with criticism over the back and sides more lengthy than the student's paper itself. On one paper which got a B, he scrawled:

I think your writing in this paper is better than your thinking
and feeling. Generally your writing is plain and clear. That
is good. But I believe you are wrong in not seeing a greater
similarity between "the father of the Bible" and "the father
of the four-room apartment home."—Also, please try to
picture a *"festering sore on the equipoise of the subsequent
family life."* Can you do it? And why weren't *you* the one
(out of 130) to wonder *why* the Prodigal Son left home in
the first place, and whether the desire for pleasure, gayety,
and beauty is a bad desire? Do you get my drift—no one was
interested in the boy until the old man ran out and fell on
his neck. But the interesting part of the son's life is in the
past.

The springtime brought Wolfe an offer from the advertising
agency with a promised stipend far greater than his teaching
salary, but he turned it down when the firm wanted him for
a minimum of three years. Occasionally he thought that the
plays might be resurrected, and the novel, now called *O Lost,*
was at last typed. *O Lost* was submitted promptly to Boni and
Liveright, who sent him a rejection slip after five weeks; Harcourt, Brace considered that the manuscript was "too long."
Meantime, Mrs. Bernstein secured the help of Madeleine Boyd
(Lulu Scudder), literary agent and wife of the writer Ernest
Boyd (Seamus Malone). Before Wolfe learned that a new publishing firm, Covici-Friede, had also rejected it, he was aboard
the *Albert Ballin* heading again for Europe. News from Asheville was that the real-estate boom had burst, his family in
difficulties.

Wolfe's six months on the Continent (June to December,
1928) were spent in restlessly moving about, in seeing new
places, and in dissipation. There was much violent drinking
and reckless conduct. It all came to a halt at the Oktoberfest
in Munich, where outside a beer hall he was attacked by several Germans who beat him so unmercifully that he was taken
to a hospital. Then in November came a letter from Scribners
signed by Maxwell Perkins (Foxhall Edwards in *You Can't Go*

Home Again), to whom Mrs. Boyd had taken the novel. "I do know," wrote Perkins, "that . . . it is a very remarkable thing, and that no editor could read it without being excited by it and filled with admiration by many passages in it. . ." With the beatific thought that at last he had found someone who could use what he had written, Wolfe sailed on the *Vulcania* from Naples.

༺ ༒ ༻

In January, 1929, he settled at 27 West 15th Street in an apartment which he again shared with Mrs. Bernstein. Like the others, it soon was laden with "papers, ledgers, books, unwashed dishes, ashes, cigarette butts, pencils and glasses. . . . Dust covered the furniture. The large studio bed near the sink always needed to be made." Over at the university he signed up for only part-time work beginning in February.

One of his first calls was at Scribners, where he heard that Perkins had been reading portions of the manuscript to Hemingway and saying that it was a "masterpiece." Already Perkins sensed that he had a Moby Dick to deal with, and then one day there was Moby Dick himself, standing "in the doorway of my boxstall of an office," wrote Perkins, "leaning against the door jamb. When I looked up and saw his wild hair and bright countenance—although he was so altogether different physically—I thought of Shelley. *He* was fair, but his hair was wild, and his face bright and his head disproportionately small." Thus began one of the most famous author-editor relationships in literature.

Perkins was known even then to be one of the most creative editors of the day. It was his quiet New England gift to see in writers a potential overlooked by his less perceptive colleagues. Though his keenness fathomed there was genius before him, he knew there was work to do and on his desk were the usual editor's notes for revisions. The work began. Mostly it was a matter of cutting material which lay outside the experience of the main character. Always annoyed with *excisions*—because *that* was the way *it* happened and the way *it* was—Wolfe never-theless agreed to the operations and even conceded Perkins was right. Organization was the problem—never did Perkins change a word or rewrite a sentence. The style, the tone, was all Wolfe's.

As the novel took final form, Wolfe began to anticipate the reaction of homefolk concerning the story he had written about them. Though he did not mail it, he dashed off a letter to the *Asheville Citizen* answering all the imaginary criticisms of his townspeople and family. He was, he feared, in for a time of trouble.

In the summer he went to Maine and Canada to read the galley proofs, and when he returned in August at the time *Scribner's Magazine* ran a section from the book called "An Angel on the Porch," he enthusiastically read his own words and was, he said, "more madly in love with myself than ever." Publication of the novel was two months away, and he went on a visit to Asheville, his last for seven years, before he started his final semester of teaching.

Publication of *Look Homeward, Angel* was set for October 18, 1929, only six days, as it happened, before the stock market panic. Though the affair with Aline Bernstein was waning, the book was dedicated "To A. B." and inscribed with the fifth stanza of John Donne's "A Valediction: On His Name in the Window." From the first, the novel was favorably received, and reviewers hailed a new talent; but the sale was not spectacu-lar. Whatever elation Wolfe received from the critics was con-siderably offset by the violence of reaction at home. The com-munity was fired with resentment that its secrets should be laid bare—its secrets and the secrets of a family exposed by one of its own sons. As Ashevillians read the pages and penciled the real names of the characters in the margins, the telephone on Spruce Street rang with sympathy and indignation. Jonathan Daniels, Wolfe's classmate at Chapel Hill, summed up the immediate reaction: "North Carolina and the South are spat upon." Only later were there time and temper to assess literary merit. From New York, where Wolfe was receiving anonymous threatening letters, he complained helplessly of those who read his work "as an almanac of personal gossip" and who tried to make it "a piece of local history." He insisted on the dignity of his creations. "There is not a single leading figure in my book who, when faced by a crisis," he wrote his mother, "does not rise up and show a heroic spirit." Concerning Eliza Gant, it should be obvious to everyone she was "a very strong, resourceful, and courageous woman, who showed great character and determination in her struggle against the odds of life."

But the wells of assumed insult were not soon filled with admiration. Wolfe began to realize there was no going home again, no turning back, even with his mother's pride—("Why that's all right, even if he calls me old Caroline Peavine. Why if he makes a success of it, I'll stand by and it'll be all right")— leading her to tour the Miami booksellers to promote her son's work. *She* was happy for him, but those home town people from whom he most wanted understanding and acclaim were not. By January, 1930, his teaching career was ended, the preliminary break with Mrs. Bernstein was made, and he had applied for a Guggenheim Fellowship. Asheville had thrown him over. Maxwell Perkins had inherited Moby Dick.

On May 10, with earned royalties of $4000 and with the Guggenheim application accepted, he sailed on the *Volendam* for Europe. In Paris he had a visit with James Boyd, the historical novelist from North Carolina, and there were pleasant times in spite of Boyd's having denounced him "before the throne of Form and Design" for *Look Homeward, Angel.* Wolfe became acquainted with F. Scott Fitzgerald (Hunt Conroy in *You Can't Go Home Again*), then in Paris, but the two could only argue about such matters as whether Americans had a homesick feeling for the land of their birth. Fitzgerald said no. Wolfe consoled himself with the thought that Fitzgerald was now "sterile and impotent and alcoholic." Fitzgerald's splendid quarters near the Bois made him uneasy. He wrote a friend in New York:

I finally departed from his company at ten that night in the
Ritz Bar where he was entirely surrounded by Princeton
boys, all nineteen years old, all drunk, and all half-raw. He
was carrying on a spirited conversation with them about
why Joe Zinzendorff did not get taken into the Triple-Gaz-
zaza Club: I heard one of the lads say "Joe's a good boy,
Scotty, but you know he's a fellow that ain't got much background."—I thought it was time for Wolfe to depart, and
I did.

No longer was Wolfe unknown in the literary world; other
authors wanted to meet him. During the autumn in London,
Sinclair Lewis (Lloyd McHarg), who in his Nobel Prize speech
had labeled *Look Homeward, Angel* as a work of "authentic
greatness," led Wolfe on a wild chase. It was a sobering experience for the younger man, now assured that fame guaranteed
only pettiness and exasperation and shallowness. He began to
despise the "literary rubbish," the autograph-seekers and party-
givers, and to execrate the Left Bank set, "life-hating, death-
living bastards." There were other troubles: the penniless family at home, losers in the real-estate crash, had to be helped.
A less-than-enthusiastic review of the English edition of *Look
Homeward, Angel* by Frank Swinnerton in the *London Evening
News* put him in a rage, and he informed Perkins that he never
intended writing again. Aline Bernstein, who did not consider
herself dismissed, sent him word that she would come after
him if he did not immediately let her know he was all right.
"But we are now at the end of the rope," he replied. "My life
has been smashed by this thing, but I am going to see if I can
get back on my feet again." Soon he was writing Perkins that
he was obsessed with the idea of getting married and settling
down.

The effect of all these aggravations was a realization that a
retreat from pressures was necessary to ward off madness. The
only hope was in his writing. He pursued a novel called "K–19"
about a train ride between Altamont and New York during
which the passengers uncovered their souls and selves. In De-

cember it dawned upon him that "no one has ever written a book about America—no one has ever put into it the things I know and the things everyone knows." Thenceforward it would be his purpose to write such a book.

In early March, 1931, Wolfe was back in New York, a city blighted by the Great Depression. Since he had only a meager income from the slow but steady sale of the novel, he retreated into the Brooklyn jungle to make his second book.

The next four years may be called the Brooklyn Years. At first he rented an apartment from the Dorman family at 40 Verandah Place ("No Door" in *From Death to Morning*). He spent little money, admitting that he "was reduced to two pairs of unmatched socks with holes in the toes, and two neckties, each embroidered with the steak and gravy of the past three years." There were periodic moves: to 111 Columbia Heights, then down the block to 101 Columbia Heights, then in 1933 to 5 Montague Terrace. All of these poorly furnished apartments looked like the ones of old, with the cigarette-burned tables, the straight chairs, the refrigerator on which he did much of his writing, and the dry-goods box in the center of the room to contain the completed pages. He had escaped into the "privacy and obscurity" which was demanded and it was a condition, he said, "I will defend with all I have." Few Brooklynites recognized or cared about the lonely six-foot-four, 235-pound man who had come to live among them.

The routine of these dismal years seldom changed. He wrote "the hard way," Edward Aswell tells us—in fits and turns, without chronology, moving from one unconnected episode to another, often revising, often rewriting entirely. In time, he deposited a thousand pages of typed manuscript with Scribners, declaring it was only half the "four-part book, or series of books" on which he was working. The day-by-day schedule generally began at eleven, when he would arise and make a pot of coffee; then he would write till early afternoon when the typist came to prepare clean copy of the manuscript; at six, after the typist had gone, he would bathe and go out to eat;

in the evening, when there were no friends about, he would push ahead until perhaps four or five in the morning. With a weekly output of fifteen or twenty thousand words, the packing case in the center of the room kept filling up. It was a lonely life, but rarely did he turn from it. A Hollywood agent who approached him was greeted with only lukewarm cordiality. His mother came to visit him; he went on a short, disappointing trip to Bermuda; and in March, 1933, he was in Washington with his family for the inauguration of Franklin D. Roosevelt. But mostly he stayed in Brooklyn and, when not writing, roamed the city streets and observed with a newly developed sympathy the Depression outcasts who slept in gutters and begged for a cup of coffee. He could have gone on like this forever, and his account of these days in *The Story of a Novel* would indicate that he wished to.

But one day late in 1933 Perkins told him his novel was complete and it must be prepared for the printer. In January the pair began going over the manuscript, page by page, with Wolfe willingly supplying connecting scenes but fiercely arguing about any cuts. After the daily two-hour meetings, at first in late afternoons and then from 8:30 to 10:30 in the evenings, they walked over to the Chatham Walk open-air bar for a drink. In June, Wolfe wrote that this association with Perkins had brought him more happiness than he had known for many years. He was relying on Perkins' "unshaken belief and friendship." This faith he wrote into the dedication of *Of Time and the River*.

The revisions in order, the job done, there was nothing to do but wait. He began to plan a vast story of America about people of a family similar to his mother's, taking them back into history and moving them westward.

There were, meanwhile, periods of doubt and fears. *Of Time and the River,* happily outlined with Perkins' help, assumed the shape of a monster which was not of his own creation. He conjured up devils which told him that Perkins had deformed his work and kept it from perfection. His troubled mind drove him to seek consolation in John Terry, a ready confidant. "We met on the street," Terry said, "stepped into a restaurant, and sat and talked for 16 hours." Wolfe would devour several big, thick, red-hot porterhouse steaks—or so the legend goes.

He could put up no longer with the terrors of his mind. A week before *Of Time and the River* was published on March 8, 1935, he sailed on the *Ile de France*. Even with financial success assured by the thirty thousand copies in print—twice the number *Look Homeward, Angel* had sold all told—he had an abnormal dread of the reviewers. In Paris, knowing the American appraisals were already in print, he walked the streets at night worrying about what they had said. Only when Perkins cabled that the novel was a triumph and that the expected comments about length and style were not unbearably harsh, was Wolfe able to calm down. In March he went over to London and got himself a Mayfair flat at 26 Hanover Square equipped with maids and a valet. As he read the dignified *Times* at breakfast, he mused how "the English have a way of putting you into an ordered and regular way of life." But he did not succumb to luxury. When he met the novelist Hugh Walpole, he was disgusted with "a man completely sold out to success" and social routine. Wolfe looked at himself, now thirty-four, and thought that his youth was gone. He pondered that the fault of artists was "not that we exceed the vital energy of life but that we fall short of it." He was determined to devote himself completely to his art. What now annoyed him most were celebrity-seekers who thrust themselves into his life and then were embittered when they were repulsed.

In May, by way of Holland, he crossed into Germany to spend the royalties accruing from the translation of *Look Homeward, Angel,* which had been vastly popular in that country but whose earning could not be sent outside. In Berlin he found he was a great personage; American Ambassador William Dodd welcomed him into his household, and daughter Martha Dodd, with the help of Wolfe's German publisher, led him off to countless engagements. It was great, but it was enervating.

He loved the German people but noticed with horror the Nazi evil "so curiously and inextricably woven into a kind of wonderful hope." After a visit to Denmark, he took passage on the *Bremen* for home, arriving July 4.

The homecoming was the most exultant moment of his life: at last, fame and success were his. Some three years later, in the last letter he ever wrote, he recalled to Maxwell Perkins how "you met me at the boat, and we went out on the café on the river and had a drink and later went on top of the tall building, and all the strangeness and the glory and the power of life and of the city was below."

In August Wolfe served on the staff of a writers' conference in Boulder, Colorado, with side trips to the Grand Canyon and New Mexico. It was his first trip West, and he was very happy. Back in New York, in an effort to capitalize on the popularity of *Of Time and the River,* Scribners was rushing through a book of his short stories, *From Death to Morning.* Perkins speeded production of the book, fearful that Wolfe would want to delay it for the insertion of stories not yet written.

In the autumn he took an apartment at 865 First Avenue overlooking the East River from fourteen stories up. Suddenly, Time was his enemy. Was there time to do all he had to do? And then the storm broke. The goddess Success exacts her payments, and Wolfe "was set upon by every kind of parasite," as he wrote, "every kind of harpy, every kind of vulture, every kind of female egotist that had a string to pull." These were the vampires who teamed up with Time to destroy him.

First of all, *Of Time and the River* had not met with the unqualified approval of his old friends any more than had *Look Homeward, Angel* with the people of Asheville. The 47 Workshop alumni took offense at the satire directed toward them and felt Wolfe had played false with Professor Baker; down at Washington Square, the book was read with dismay at the abuse heaped upon his erstwhile well-wishers. Apparently neither group had any understanding of Wolfe's fictional intent.

Secondly, a trio of lawsuits popped up to stir the serenity

he needed for his writing. Madeleine Boyd maintained she was still his agent for *Of Time and the River* and sued for $10,000. When the case was finally settled for $500, Wolfe added $150 after listening to the lawyers' tales of Mrs. Boyd's "hard luck." A more serious matter was the libel suit by the Dorman family with whom Wolfe had lived at 40 Verandah Place, Brooklyn. In "No Door," it was maintained, one of the characters, easily identified, was so presented that she was personally, adversely affected. Wolfe was incensed, and Perkins argued that he ought to settle out of court to give himself some peace of mind, if nothing more. But the case dragged on and when a settlement was finally made, Wolfe's share in the loss was $2745.25. Believing he could have won eventually, he blamed Scribners for his financial downfall.

The last case concerned a young New Jersey man whose family had befriended Terry and Wolfe. Out of a job, Murdock Dooher asked to be Wolfe's agent in the sale of his manuscripts. A number were turned over to him but, when the lad burned some of them and pocketed the cash from others without making any payment, Wolfe, this time, was forced to take the initiative in the courts. He won, but the victory left sordid fingerprints.

Other provoking incidents plagued him: he claimed he had received blackmail letters; he had troubles about speaking engagements. Though he wanted merely to be left alone, no one seemed willing to let him go his way. Finally, the climax to this series of irritabilities came over the royalty to be paid for *The Story of a Novel* (1936). In his first grave quarrel with Scribners, Wolfe fumed when Perkins suggested that 10 per cent, instead of the usual 15 per cent, was right for so small a book. Perkins quickly gave in, but Wolfe was hardly placated, even though he wrote Perkins that "all the damn contracts in the world don't mean as much to me as your friendship does." When Bernard De Voto wrote in his review of *The Story of a Novel* that "the assembly-line at Scribners" could hardly help Wolfe to master his material, the novelist justly felt his integrity as a writer had been questioned. It was true, fame was a shadow, devotion to art a cipher, and acclaim a thing of straw. Two days before De Voto's gloomy words were printed, Wolfe was darkly reflecting that there was "something a little grotesque and tragic in the fact that the success I wanted and looked forward to having as a child should have brought me so much trouble, worry, bewilderment and disillusion. . ."

To avoid for a while the mockery and the law courts, he frequently escaped the city. In March, 1936, he went south for the first time since *Look Homeward, Angel*. Returning from New Orleans, he stopped by Chapel Hill and Raleigh, but was not yet willing to face the uncertainty of Asheville. In May he went down to York Springs, near Gettysburg, looking for information on his father's people. In July he made a seventh and last trans-Atlantic voyage. His German publishers had funds wating for him at Bremerhaven. In Berlin, amid the pomp of the Olympic games, he realized that Europe was ready to erupt ("I Have a Thing To Tell You" in *You Can't Go Home Again*) and that everyone must concern himself with politics if the world would be saved. In October he was back in New York.

At this point a severance of his publishing relationship with Scribners was inevitable. Perkins knew that in time Wolfe would write up the "story" of the Scribner days and that he, along with his associates, would be in one of the Wolfe novels. A New England terror of publicity troubled him. Too, he and Wolfe were divided on ideological issues (the last four chapters of *You Can't Go Home Again*) ; and Perkins protested when Wolfe wished to replace his lyrical prose with arguments, political and ethical. So, with a cry of anguish the writer forsook his friend, as he had forsaken others—Professor Baker, Aline Bernstein—because though he depended on others, he could not bear to feel the weight of that dependence. He had to be free, free to write without even the slightest awareness of patronage or intervention. The shy and uncomprehending Perkins wrote to Wolfe:

I can't express certain kinds of feelings very comfortably,
but you must realize what my feelings are toward you. Ever
since "Look Homeward, Angel" your work has been the foremost interest in my life, and I have never doubted for your
future on any grounds except, at times, on those of your
being able to control the vast mass of material you have ac-
cumulated and have to form into books. You seem to think
I have tried to control you. I only did that when you asked
my help and then I did the best I could.

Later he reminded Wolfe that the assistance was only "me-
chanical," a fact which Wolfe seemed to have forgotten. "You
were never overruled. Do you think you are clay to be
moulded! I never saw anyone less malleable." But the past
was broken beyond healing. Frantically Wolfe began searching
for another editor, another publisher.

❧ ☙

When he could afford it, he fled the iniquitous city. In January, 1937, he was once again in North Carolina, and in the
spring he took off down the Shenandoah Valley and into Yancey
County, just northeast of Asheville. There he was eager to talk
with John Westall, his maternal grandfather's half-brother, and
to note the old tales for subsequent use in his novels. From
forty-five miles away, he wondered if he dared go home, dared
to return after seven years. Would a native son be welcomed
who had "disgraced" his family and his townspeople? When
determination won over dread, he made his way across the
mountain and, from the first moment, he discovered to his un-
belief that he was "a crashing success." The city had forgiven
him, he was a celebrity. During his ten days or so there, he
rented an isolated cabin at Oteen, six miles from Asheville, and
planned to return in the summer.

For two months, July and August, he settled on the hilltop,
hired a colored boy as servant, and worked on "The Party at
Jack's" (in *You Can't Go Home Again*). At first there was much
fun and there were no intruders, just family and close friends.

Usually he worked all day, then had dinner in the evening with his mother at the Old Kentucky Home, now seldom crowded with roomers. By August, however, the cabin had turned into a three-ring circus, he later said. Asheville desired to honor him, the tourists wished to gaze at a real live author, and the young social set wanted to brighten his evenings with drinking and merrymaking. It was all no use; Wolfe retreated into a downtown Asheville hotel incognito and eventually slipped away.

After a short visit with the writer Anne W. Armstrong in the Tennessee mountains, he stopped overnight with Sherwood Anderson in Virginia before heading back to New York. Unaware of the strained relations between author and editor, Anderson wrote Perkins:

> Tom Wolfe has been here to see us. I'm afraid we didn't have a bed in the house long enough for him. The man is a flood, a continent, but he is generous and full of fine feeling.
>
> He seems worried and upset, uncertain about the future. He seems to want so much, marriage among other things. Max, you'd better marry Tom off, get him a shrewd woman who will keep him out of trouble.
>
> The man has tremendous gifts. He only stayed over the night and through most of the next day and then went on to Roanoke. . .

In the autumn Wolfe rented a three-room suite, Room 807, at the Hotel Chelsea on West 23rd Street, an old plush establishment once frequented by Mark Twain and O. Henry. His interlude at the Oteen mountain cabin had been a failure. He wrote his brother Fred: "I guess that's the end of me in Asheville. . . . I've just found out a man must stand alone." Now he had no faith but in his work; he kept his address a secret and saw no one except his agent, Elizabeth Nowell, and a few guests of the hotel like Edgar Lee Masters.

The Chelsea suite had high ceilings, ancient but comfortable furniture, and an amazing toilet perched on a high platform in the bathroom. The familiar packing cases filled the center area

49

of the sitting room—a depository not only of manuscript but "pots and pans, old shoes, stacks of letters and receipted bills, discarded hats, useless knickknacks people had given him, a flat iron, in short everything which he . . . could not bear to part with." This is the description of Edward C. Aswell of Harpers, who often visited him there as his new editor. In November, Wolfe was offered a contract with Harpers providing for an advance of $10,000 against 15 per cent royalty. Wolfe was not displeased, for Harpers was an old house, and Aswell a young Southerner from Nashville who, Wolfe said, "thinks I am the best writer in the country."

At the Chelsea he worked solidly through the winter, only occasionally interrupting his work to disport with the literary crowd at the hotel. Aswell was a frequent caller and observed the way he went about his writing. Wolfe would pace the rooms, his fingers tearing at his hair, his mind rehearsing some episode he had turned over dozens of times. When he had got it straight, he put on his glasses (for he now wore them), sat at the table, and the words poured rapidly and effortlessly from his pencil onto the yellow paper. After the typist had assembled and transcribed the pages, Wolfe would revise and often rewrite whole scenes. The packing cases filled up. "I am having to begin my education all over again," he wrote his sister Mabel. Convinced he could not change the world, he nevertheless could and would "work for a better one, and in that direction lies hope and new life, and not defeat."

In the spring, he was fed up with New York. He went down to Baltimore to see the writer Gerald Johnson, like Wolfe originally from North Carolina, with the idea of going there to live. Johnson took him to a real-estate agent who drove him about, but nothing came of it. Meanwhile, he had been invited to lecture at Purdue University. He was tired and decided to move on from Purdue to the West Coast for a vacation. So, with the help of a secretary, he took his vast manuscript from the packing cases and began arranging it in the "most logical and accurate sequence." Aswell came by to offer his aid, for the agreement was for Aswell to familiarize himself with the material while Wolfe was gone. The two of them planned later to dig at it the way Perkins and Wolfe had done. Aswell took the manuscript away—typed pages "breast high from the floor," much of it rewritten versions of the same incidents, and discarded sections from the already published books. On May 17 Wolfe left New York.

It was a happy holiday: first Purdue, then Chicago, and on to the West. In June he accepted the invitation of two news-papermen to accompany them on a two-week automobile tour of national parks. Since Wolfe had never learned to drive a car, he had ample time to fill his eyes with the wonders of western America, and every night before retiring he wrote in a ledger the fresh impressions of the day (published as *A Western Journal*).

In early July, on a trip to British Columbia, he contracted pneumonia, but the crisis quickly passed after hospitalization in Seattle. When a fever persisted during convalescence, the doc-tors had an X ray taken which "revealed an unresolved condi-tion of the upper lobe of the right lung . . . diagnosed as an old tubercular lesion." Mabel Wheaton arrived in Seattle and set out by train with her brother and a nurse for Johns Hopkins Hospital. They were joined by Julia Wolfe at Chicago. In Balti-more an operation showed that Wolfe's brain was infected by tubercular germs released during the siege with pneumonia.

Thomas Wolfe died on September 15, 1938, eighteen days short of his thirty-eighth birthday. Funeral services were held at the First Presbyterian Church of Asheville, and he was buried in Riverside Cemetery there. He had, of course, come home at last —a home which he had set "down in love, in contempt, in beauty and in ugliness," wrote Jonathan Daniels. "He drew his land as it was and wise men will rejoice for the drawing." The feud was over, his "sins" were forgiven.

An early will dividing his estate between his mother and Aline Bernstein had been revised on April 17, 1937, leaving everything to his family. Maxwell Perkins was named executor and so he remained, despite the break with Scribners. In truth, the admiration of the author for his greatest friend, and the admiration of the editor for his protégé, never slackened. When Perkins knew Wolfe was to die, he kept saying over in his mind the lines from *King Lear*:

> He hates him
> That would upon the rack of this tough world
> Stretch him out longer.

"For," wrote Perkins, "he was on the rack almost always, and almost always would have been—and for one reason. He was wrestling as no artist in Europe would have to do, with the material of literature—a great country not yet revealed to its own people."

Wolfe had not won, but he had made a beginning.

3

ᵉᵇ "LOOK HOMEWARD, ANGEL"

Usually the first book of a young writer is a book of discovery. From his meager experience, accentuated by his youth, comes a knowledge so new and so startling and so wonderful that its pain is almost beyond bearing. Mellow, many-faceted understanding is not for now; understanding is the hard reward of decades of summers. Youth's knowledge, youth's discoveries, are as sure as an April dawn.

Look Homeward, Angel was written out of a need for discovery as well as a need for assessing the knowledge of a young man. By 1926 Thomas Wolfe had found out many things, but only through a creative act could his knowledge be refined into truth. For artists, it has always been so.

Wolfe was in England that summer, at loose ends. At night he lay in his bed remembering he had been born in North Carolina and wondering why he was then in England. The writing began in the first person. Later the name "Eugene" would have to be substituted for the pronoun "I." Before the first draft was completed, seventeen large ledgers would be filled with his generous scrawl. Creation demanded sixty cigarettes a day, twenty cups of coffee, food gulped down whenever he could manage to tear himself away from the ledgers and whenever he happened to recall he was hungry—or so Wolfe wrote of his author-hero in *You Can't Go Home Again*. The writing proceeded without any appraisal of the results, "in simpleness and nakedness of soul," he said, with a "child's innocency and wonder."

What was the book about? A month after its publication Wolfe tried to make clear to his mother that its theme was clearly stated in the opening pages: "that we are born alone—all of us who ever lived or will live—that we live alone, and die alone, and that we are strangers to one another, and never come to know one another."

That the novel is autobiographical is apparent but, then, Wolfe thought that all worthwhile fiction is autobiographical. It could be no other way, for every man is his own center and all he knows comes from his experience. But that the novel is *fact* was not true. A writer might create one character out of a hundred persons whom he had known. Fiction was, he defined, only "fact selected and understood . . . arranged and charged with purpose," and the world Wolfe created was always inside him, never outside. If the people in his book had their basis in human experience, the life and being they possessed was only what he himself gave them.

The plot of *Look Homeward, Angel*—perhaps *plan* is the better word—corresponds roughly with the first twenty years of Wolfe's life. In 1900, at the Southern mountain town of Altamont in the state of Old Catawba, Eugene Gant was born, the eighth child and the fifth son of an itinerant Pennsylvania father and a hill-born mother. The union of William Oliver Gant and Eliza Pentland Gant had, from the beginning, been a stormy one. The father was a romantic, poetry-quoting stone-cutter, while the mother was primarily of a practical turn of mind. The night Eugene was born, Gant had been on a glorious drunk. As the child grew up, he along with his brothers and

Original Angel, Hendersonville, N.C.

University of North Carolina Library

sisters was caught hopelessly in the crosscurrents. He knew he would always be the sad, the lost one, "imprisoned in that beating and most secret heart." From his earliest moments of consciousness, memory folded back upon him and the "bell rang under the sea."

When not quite six, Eugene began public schooling. His brothers and sisters, who thought him "queer," had little time for him. Almost at once he learned to read, and then to write. In the first grade he still had curls which his mother could not bear to clip, and the pack of wolves at the school, sensing a stranger among them, mercilessly persecuted him. In the third grade he was writing little poems and stuffing them in his desk. As for games, he never learned to play them or to be part of a team.

At home, Eliza, grieving over the death of her son Grover at the World's Fair in St. Louis, nevertheless pushed the brothers into the street to earn money selling newspapers and magazines. W. O. continued his periodic brawls, making no secret of his frequent visits to the local brothel. Soon, Eliza opened up Dixieland, a boarding house, and with her went Eugene. His sister Helen stayed behind with her father at the old house, the other children—Daisy, Steve, Ben, and Luke—moving restlessly between the two but mainly eating at Eliza's table. Eugene hated Dixieland, was ashamed of it, and felt he had lost not only social caste and dignity but all the essence of privacy.

The duality of his life began to shape the lad. Though his mother's conduct affronted him, he recognized the kinship, even so, and shared with her the potency of memory and talk, and a "powerful clairvoyance, the wild Scotch gift." His sensory impressions developed so keenly that "at the moment of perception of a single thing, the whole background of color, warmth, odor, sound, taste established itself." His father, he admiringly thought, was not a mere maker of tombstones, but a master craftsman of enduring works which would prevent his being forgotten when he died. In the lost area between these two dominating but conflicting forces, Eugene wanted to gain the love he did not have and he wanted to be famous. These ambitions were not unlike those of all who were ever born.

The last four years of his preparatory training were spent at a private school operated by John and Margaret Leonard. John was a spiritless creature, but Margaret, upon the foundation of Eugene's love of books, brought the boy to literature. With Margaret, for the first time he was able to reveal to someone else the buried life which he lived. Not even to Ben, whom he loved above all others, could he open a window.

Just before his sixteenth birthday, Eugene entered the state university at Pulpit Hill. His first year was painful and lonely, pressed within himself as he was by a hostile world of hostile students who made fun of his strange tall figure. Thereafter he gradually managed to bear the taunts and even play up to the howlings of the merrymakers. But Wolfe does not deal minutely with Eugene's college years. Most of the chapters are anecdotal: a visit to a prostitute in a nearby town, an incident in a Latin class, and so on. What is more clearly detailed is the boy's inner life, his alternate elation and dejection, the development of a centaur-cry which tried "to unburden its overladen heart in one blast of pain and joy and passion." By the end of his senior year, Eugene had conquered the visible enemy, he had become a big man on the campus, but the gnawing from within was still there. Even at the pinnacle of campus success, Eugene sensed that his fellows, most of whom were little more than industrious, mediocre hacks, "safe, sound, and reliable," resented his brilliance.

Three episodes punctuate this section of the novel. During the first summer vacation Eugene fell in love with Laura James, a boarder at his mother's Dixieland. Without acknowledging her engagement to be married, the older girl led him into a love which was young, innocent, and beautiful, ironically blooming within a setting of drunkenness and cheap humanity. The picnic scene, concluding with the rich prose-poem "Come up into the hills, O my young love," is followed by Eugene's lonely agony at the realization of her defection.

A second episode was his journey to Norfolk to help in the national effort during the height of World War I. It was there, in a period of sweat and awkward misdirection, that he knew he could survive on his own, and more and more he sought escape from family and home town.

The third concerned the illness and death of Ben during the influenza epidemic of 1918. With the sympathetic Ben gone, Eugene felt there was no longer any reason to remain encased within the imprisoning mountains. In that final lyric chapter, he discussed with the ghost of Ben a journey out, and Ben told him that a man's world is himself. Even so, Eugene was determined to leave on the next day. He was twenty years old.

❧ ☙

Such a bare and inadequate outline gives no hint of the opulence of *Look Homeward, Angel*. Besides Eugene, there are in the novel several characters monumental in their graphic individuality and personality. Those most unforgettable are Gant, Eliza, Ben, and Helen.

William Oliver Gant is memorable chiefly because he had a tremendous gusto for life. No passive figure, he was either violent in denunciation or ecstatic in approval. To his family, in spite of his comic vulgarity, he brought a ritual which gave a pattern to their days. The children loved him for being a good provider; he brought home whole carcasses of meat, huge baskets of farm produce; at breakfast he heaped their plates "with great slabs of fried steak, grits fried in egg, hot biscuits, jam, fried apples"; he had a love of abundance. He was lusty in his speech, covering Eliza with abuse at one moment, in the next railing aloud some Shakespearean lines in inebriated glory. He was sensual, moving from wife to wife, spawning numbers of children, assaulting Negro cooks, and indiscriminately showing himself at Queen Elizabeth's "house." Yet, though he loved his home and his brood, he was the Far-Wanderer with a nomad's hunger for voyages—the hunger that haunts all Americans, Wolfe wrote, and makes us homeless strangers. If a symbol be needed, Gant's life was like a river, the Mississippi River, "rich with its own deposited and onward-borne agglutinations, fecund with its sedimental accretions, filled exhaustlessly by life in order to be more richly itself." The thing which obstructed the flow was Eliza's Dixieland, "this damnable, this awful, this murderous and bloody Barn." There amid the chattering, gluttonous boarders he felt most alone and lost. Gant was dying slowly of cancer, but no one would tell him, and he would not give up.

The character of Eliza is more complex. The mountains of her birth gave her independence and energy and pride, plus a minstrel's flair for storing old stories away in her mind for eventual recounting. In unhurried dips into memory, she took her time, pulling into byways and exploring the paths of events till all was swept clean. She was egocentric without being egotistical; she was dependent on the love of her family without surrendering her native freedom. When life turned against her in the form of an unhappy, unfortunate marriage, Eliza gathered to herself other symbols of security—"old string, empty cans and bottles, paper, trash of every description." If her acquisitiveness angered her husband and children, she did not bother to explain, or perhaps she did not know, the real reasons for her frugality. The change came in her at the time when Eugene was weaned at the age of three. "Something in her stopped," Wolfe wrote; "something began." The death of Grover the following year left her, as other disappointments left the other members of her family, a lost person. From that point on, it is all too easy to blame Eliza for the disasters which followed one another—the splitting of the family, for instance, and Eugene's efforts to escape, and Ben's death—but beneath the exterior was a generous, noble woman compensating for the buffets of fortune in the only way left to her. Wolfe thought of her that way. If personal relationships had no meaning, money and property did have one. Her cross lay in her family's lack of understanding, not in any spiritual or moral weakness.

59

Ben, with the gray eyes, the bumpy skin, the shapely head, and the perpetual scowl, had with Eugene a kinship outside the family circle. Apparently only Ben had any knowledge of the boy's problems. This was true because he, like Eugene, was always trying "to find some entrance into life, some secret undiscovered door—a stone, a leaf—that might admit him into light and fellowship." He never found the door, but there was ever, as Wolfe puts it, the sound of the lost world and the great forgotten language. In the absence of earth-bound communication, Ben talked to his Demon. Eliza, delivering some of her practical advice, would be countered by Ben's cocking his head up to his dark angel and exclaiming, "Oh, my God. Listen to that!" As Eugene knew and observed, he spoke to his angel quickly and often. If the chapters on Ben's death have been said to be one of the great death scenes in all literature, the opinion is due in large measure to Wolfe's writing of one of the most profound experiences a young man ever had. For Eugene, it was the death of recognition.

Alongside these tragic portrayals, Wolfe drew a warm picture of Helen, unsparing, big-boned, open-hearted. She was the solid one amid the otherwise uncertain family ties, and it seemed to be a need within her to throw away her boundless energies in service for her family. She was always there when she was wanted, complaining maybe, but intensifying her efforts to negate the complaints. Helen's intense love for her father was her signal of self-denial. She could not bear to leave him in the less sympathetic hands of Eliza. She was like her father in lustiness, abundance, and raucous humor. But Helen, unlike the others, was not lost.

Daisy, Steve, and Luke, individual though they were, are less vividly presented; yet they, too, with all their strengths and weaknesses, often seem oversized and godlike in a primal world. Outside the Gant family the characters shrink into everyday proportions.

Wolfe's desire was not, however, merely to write a novel telling of the pains of youth surrounded by people who either were incapable of understanding or were powerless to help. His intention was far greater, and perhaps if one is to get at this intention, he ought to look closely at the clues Wolfe has provided.

Look Homeward, Angel carries as its subtitle "A Story of the Buried Life." What did Wolfe mean by this? Evidently the phrase was borrowed from Matthew Arnold's short poem beginning "Light flows our war of mocking words," in which Arnold comments on that part of man's life hidden behind the disguises he wears and on his inability, except in moments of love, to reveal himself. This buried life, even so, is the real one, the essential one which lends meaning to existence. Wolfe extended this notion into what he called his "plan" for the book. Before the novel was accepted for publication, he wrote that in it "There are two essential movements—one outward and one downward. The outward movement describes the effort of a child, a boy, and a youth for release, freedom, and loneliness in new lands. . . . The downward movement is represented by a constant excavation into the buried life of a group of people, and describes the cyclic curve of a family's life—genesis, union, decay, and dissolution." The buried life was a secret life, and though even Gant and Eliza had such a side, it is mainly Eugene, and to a lesser degree, Ben, who are shown to be strangers to the world.

With Eugene the secret life had much to do with imagination, by means of which he daydreamed of huge ships and faraway cities and lands which opened out. In his imagination there was belief in the great virtues: tenderness and gentleness, beauty and love and goodness, valiance and glory. There were more intense moments like the one in which he lusciously imagined himself the only male in a town of pretty women whence all the men had fled, and how he would loot the shops and cellars and fulfill all his sensuous desires. There were more comical moments in which he saw himself as "Ace Gant, the falcon of

61

the skies, with 63 Huns to his credit by his nineteenth year." And there were the more honest moments when he admitted "the wild confusion of adolescence, the sexual nightmares of puberty, the grief, the fear, the shame in which a boy broods over the dark world of his desire," when "every boy, caged in from confession by his fear, is to himself a monster."

The essence of the buried life was a continuation of prenatal existence. If Wolfe borrowed Arnold's phrase for his subtitle, he was even more influenced by the Neoplatonic romanticism of Wordsworth and Coleridge. In the prose-poem facing the first chapter are these well remembered words: "Naked and alone we came into exile. In her dark womb we did not know our mother's face; from the prison of her flesh have we come into the unspeakable and incommunicable prison of this earth." Eugene was born trailing Wordsworthian clouds of glory, but all too soon he was suspended in time, caught in life's prison-house, and the sound of the great bell ringing underseas was dimmer and dimmer. As time went on, the prison house became more stifling, and though he sought to escape the prison gates, he came to realize that his incarceration was complete and he found comfort in the fantasy of the buried life. Thus walled in, he projected "an acceptable counterfeit of himself which would protect him from intrusion." At birth he knew the word— "the lost key opening the prison gates, the lane-end into heaven"—but eventually, like all who are born, he forgot it.

Re-echoes of pre-existence and the buried life persist throughout the novel and give it unity. To go a step further, Albrecht contends that Wolfe utilized, besides the pre-existence-and-return myth, other Platonic contrasts: dark and light, many and one, isolation and union, imprisonment and freedom, shadow and reality. His study and love of the romantic poets left their mark.

While the subtitle and opening sentences of *Look Homeward, Angel* established a mood for the story to follow, they do not state a theme. Almost from the first days when Wolfe started writing the novel, there was no doubt in his mind what his intent would be. Though the materials would come from his own life, he planned to tell, he wrote Mrs. Roberts, "the story of a powerful creative element trying to work its way toward an essential isolation; a creative solitude; a secret life—its fierce struggles to wall this part of its life away from birth, first against the public and savage glare of an unbalanced, nervous brawling family group; later against school, society, all the barbarous invasions of the world." The words are clear. Wolfe was then twenty-five years old; his young spirit was being assailed by the world which he had sought outside his mountains; he needed at that moment for the past to be caught, as it was with Proust, through memory; and he felt the necessity to put down on paper the agony of his present problem.

The pith of any work of fiction is conflict. Eugene Gant's conflict was one between himself and world, between himself and family, school, and society. He struggled against a father whose artistic nature he thought had been wasted, against a mother whose love he believed he had lost, against brothers and sisters who had succumbed to the pressures and been defeated. Inwardly he took up arms against a home town which he felt was united to destroy him. He was determined to keep his individuality intact.

Eugene's fight is all the more difficult because he was constantly aware that, in spite of his strong resolution to preserve his self, the elements of Chance were operating full time. Eugene had only to go back in memory to know that "the loss or gain of a moment, the turn of the head, the enormous and aimless impulsion of accident, had thrust into the blazing heat of him." And so it would go on, each moment being the culmination of thousands and thousands of years. Cause led on to Cause, and Man's life was not ordered by mind and reason but was the frenzied fumbling of Chance, Variety, and Fate. If the battle was unequal, the best one could do was to isolate himself —to "wall" himself in—and "escape" into life, not from it.

Like all young men, Eugene pondered the reasons why life should be this way, but these occasions were rare. Generally they came in fancied seconds when Time was suspended and no-Time took over. Eugene would see a woman from a train window, and suddenly the train was motionless, the woman was frozen without movement, and Time was stopped. The reader of *Look Homeward, Angel* may recall that the instant after W. O. Gant had sold the angel to Queen Elizabeth, he stood upon the steps of his stonecutter's shop and the pulsing fountain in the public square was held in photographic fixity. Where was man headed? "Where now? Where after? Where then?" There was no answer. Only death was sure.

∽ ∾

Throughout the novel, the mood and theme are enriched by a number of symbols which must be understood if the poetic nature of the fiction is to be fully realized. A translation of poetic symbols is not always easy, and the reason is aptly given by Richard Chase in *The American Novel and Its Tradition*:

> . . . a poetic symbol not only *means* something, it *is* something—namely, an autonomous truth which has been discovered in the process by which the symbol emerged in the context of the poem. If it still permits us to think of it as an ordinary symbol—as something that stands for something else—we see that it does not point to anything easy to express. Rather, it suggests several meanings. . . . Furthermore, the "poetry" of a novel will probably reside less in the language than in the rhythm and relation of picture, scene, character, and action . . .

This is especially true of Wolfe, where the symbolic words *are* something at the same time they carry another intention. Moreover, like the whale in Melville, the intention is constantly shifting, rarely static.

A good example is the Angel of the title. Here are the lines from Milton's "Lycidas":

> Or whether thou [the poet's college friend who has drowned],
>   to our moist vows denied,

64

Sleep'st by the fable of Bellerus old,
Where the great Vision of the guarded mount
Looks toward Namancos and Bayona's hold.
Look homeward, Angel, now, and melt with ruth:
And, O ye dolphins, waft the hapless youth.

Here Milton invokes the protector angel St. Michael to turn
from foreign threats in order to weep for a disaster at home.
The same meaning may be applied to Wolfe's novel. Heaven is
urged to look toward home and "melt with ruth" rather than
gaze afar for tragic possibilities. Altamont and the Gant family
have their own pathetic lives. This poetic interpretation of the
word *angel* is balanced by a palpable image: the stone angel on
the porch of Gant's shop. This angel, which Wolfe wrote was
responsible for his title, "had come from Carrara in Italy, and
it held a stone lily delicately in one hand. The other hand was
lifted in benediction, it was poised clumsily upon the ball of
one phthisic foot, and its stupid white face wore a smile of soft
stone idiocy." As a youth in Baltimore, Gant had seen such an
angel and had then yearned to carve a similar one and thus
release evidence of the creative urge within him. He never
learned to carve such an angel; the artistic impulse burned
and died as the prisonhouse closed about him in the philistine
confines of Altamont. In this instance, the angel is the symbol
of the creativity which, though throbbing, is suppressed in most
men.

A third and more compelling interpretation, and in no way
unconnected with the other two, is the angel of Ben and Eugene.
Wolfe generally substituted the word ghost, the ghost being the
spirit from some pre-existence. "O lost, and by the wind grieved,
ghost, come back again," Wolfe reiterated. The ghost is a lonely
spirit. It is sometimes synonymous with the loss of innocence
as when, after Eugene's first visit to a prostitute, he "was
haunted by his own lost ghost: he knew it to be irrecoverable."
But the angel-ghost image, like any wraith, shifts and changes.
Often it stands for corporeal life, which is not real at all, but

65

a zombie taking the place of the real. At such times the ghost wails for a return into life from exile. The ghost therefore is lost. Eugene, himself a ghost, seeks the way of returning. "The way is here, Eugene. Have you forgotten? The leaf, the rock, the wall of light. Lift up the rock, Eugene, the leaf, the stone, the unfound door. Return, return." Then, after Ben's death, Ben *becomes* Eugene's ghost, and Ben's answer to the question "Where is the world?" is the simple one "*You* are your world." In that last chapter, the dead Ben finally has life, and he is therefore no longer a ghost. The stone angels begin to move, and with them Eugene believes himself freed. The ghost-angel reappears as creative power. (See Albrecht's "Time as Unity.")

Often in the same context as the angel is the triple symbol "a stone, a leaf, a door." In *The Prelude*, Wordsworth writes of "a tree, a stone, a withered leaf," a phrasing upon which Wolfe apparently based his refrain. In his novels, the *stone* is reminiscent of Gant's angel and its metaphorical meaning for the artist; it is also the solid element in life's uncertain transformations. The *leaf*—the "withered leaf"—is, by way of contrast, consonant with decay and death. The most frequently used of the three words is the *door*, and the search for the door, which, if one could find and enter it, would mean artistic and spiritual fulfillment.

There are many other ringing words, of course. The train, with its apostrophe to America and to America's unknown people and places, sometimes becomes for Eugene the "gateway to the lost world." More than any other symbol, the train is Wolfe's signature, as the star is Robert Frost's.

And there are the mountains, which represent Eugene's bound-in life and his desire for escape.

All of these symbols are tied in with Wolfe's mood and theme, culminating in Eugene's conviction "that men do not escape from life because life is dull, but that life escapes from men because men are little."

The symbols are interwoven into the prose paragraphs, and when the reader comes upon them, they are like the soft low notes of a musical instrument, sounding to remind him that outside the story of written words is a meaning deeper and more profound than the progressive narrative before him.

❧ ❧

Wolfe's search for America is less evident in *Look Homeward, Angel* than in the later books. In his first novel he was so concerned with an examination of his youth that he had not yet projected his subject matter very far beyond Altamont and Old Catawba. The country out there was largely *terra incognita*. Still there are hints that the stretch of America was in his mind. Gant's trip to California by train called forth a rhapsodic passage. When Eugene takes a trip down into South Carolina (by train, of course), there in the nighttime beyond the windows was "the American earth—rude, immeasurable, formless, mighty."

If the quest of America was yet to come, not so Wolfe's discovery of poetry. Fully does *Look Homeward, Angel* deserve the rather generally agreed-upon opinion that it is the most lyrical novel ever written by an American. There are many ways in which Wolfe used poetry. Besides the rhythmic lines, the colorful phrasing, the symbolic images, and the leitmotifs, Wolfe picked up from Joyce a method of using well-known phrases from classical poetry, verbatim or in paraphrase, to balance Eugene's everyday world. In this fashion was Eugene able to rout his enemies in secret and to comment upon the commonplace. For instance, noticing a streetcleaner at his vulgar labor (in that most Joycean of chapters, number 24), the boy's mind runs to Gray's line, "Let not Ambition mock their useful toil." Taunted by his friend's reasoning that it paid to be a Christian because church membership was good for business, Eugene thinks with Coleridge: "To walk together to the kirk, with a goodly company."

Such a scheme is not, of course, inherently poetic. More to the point is the chapter on Ben's funeral (number 37), where Wolfe leaves prose far behind, and even poetry merges into music. Like the last scene of *Götterdämmerung,* a whole symphony of themes is repeated and pulsed toward the transcendent triumph of life over death.

In the last chapter, the meeting of Eugene with Ben's ghost provides Wolfe with an opportunity to drift into pure fantasy; and to match the fantasy are the cadenced phrases and suggestive terms. "I shall lift no stone upon the hills," Eugene says to the ghost in nonrealistic expression; "I shall find no door in any city. But in the city of myself, upon the continent of my soul, I shall find the forgotten language, the lost world, a door where I may enter, and music strange as any ever sounded; I shall haunt you, ghost, along the labyrinthine ways until— until? O Ben, my ghost, an answer?"

Wolfe's use of poetry must take into account, too, his dithyrambic paragraphs which delight in sensuous impressions. Sound and sight passages are not unusual in prose fiction, but Wolfe is one of the few writers for whom the pleasures of smell can be prolonged for page after page. All the senses are keenly at work in his descriptions of food, in which sections even Dickens is rivaled. Here is a delectable account succinctly covering a day at the Gant household:

> In the morning they rose in a house pungent with breakfast cookery, and they sat at a smoking table loaded with brains and eggs, ham, hot biscuit, fried apples seething in their gummed syrups, honey, golden butter, fried steak, scalding coffee. Or there were stacked batter-cakes, rum-colored molasses, fragrant brown sausages, a bowl of wet cherries, plums, fat juicy bacon, jam. At the mid-day meal, they ate heavily: a huge hot roast of beef, fat buttered lima-beans, tender corn smoking on the cob, thick red slabs of sliced tomatoes, rough savory spinach, hot yellow corn-bread, flaky biscuits, a deep-dish peach and apple cobbler spiced with cinnamon, tender cabbage, deep glass dishes piled with preserved fruits—cherries, pears, peaches. At night they might eat fried steak, hot squares of grits fried in egg and butter, pork-chops, fish, young fried chicken.

The Old Kentucky Home, Asheville, about 1914

69

If such a passage is less than lyric poetry, it must be remembered that Wolfe had many styles at his command. Poetry and realism are inextricably compounded in the slice-of-life portions of the book, especially when they concern the early morning activities of various folk in Altamont. At such times Wolfe wrote in Joycean sentences to his heart's content.

When in a jolly mood, Wolfe could turn to parody and, particularly when he was telling of Eugene's daydreams, mock the sentimental fiction which went for literature in Altamont. Or he could ridicule the stupid social-column writing of the newspaper, as here:

> "Members of the Younger Set were charmingly entertained last night at a dinner dance given at Snotwood, the beautiful residence of Mr. and Mrs. Clarence Firkins, in honor of their youngest daughter, Gladys, who made her debutt this season. Mr. and Mrs. Firkins, accompanied by their daughter, greeted each of the arriving guests at the threshold in a manner reviving the finest old traditions of Southern aristocracy, while Mrs. Firkins' accomplished sister, Miss Catherine Hipkiss, affectionately known to members of the local younger set as Roaring Kate, supervised the checking of overcoats, evening wraps, jockstraps, and jewelry . . ."

The account continues in this vein, but the paragraph is enough to toss to the winds the claims of those who affirm that Wolfe was without humor.

The central and simplest theme of *Look Homeward, Angel* is the revolt of the individual from the small town, a theme uppermost in the minds of other writers of the 1920's—Zona Gale, Sherwood Anderson, and Sinclair Lewis, to name a few. But unlike the works of these authors, *Look Homeward, Angel* was written at a time when the clouds of glory had not entirely passed away, at a time before the prison house had completely closed in. The stars were right; the union of Boy and Man was as nearly perfect as could ever be expected, and from this union came a lyrical quality rare in fiction.

When the work was finished, Wolfe was sure in his mind that one did not write a book to keep it forever in his memory. One writes a book to forget it. There were other experiences and other tasks, and so he turned to them.

4

ᴈ§ "OF TIME AND THE RIVER"

Aᴏᴛᴇʀ his first novel was published, Wolfe had no clear notion of the sort of book that was to follow it. He tried several ideas unsuccessfully, but eventually settled upon the inevitable: a continuation of Eugene Gant's adventures. If *Look
Homeward, Angel* was written in a dawnlike flush of discovery,
not so *Of Time and the River,* which came when Wolfe's productive powers were at their peak. So excessive was the flower-
ing, in fact, that he had difficulty controlling the unforced
rush of words. An account of this period may be found in *The
Story of a Novel,* where he writes of his work pouring "from
him for almost five years like burning lava from a volcano."
Much of this intemperate overflow was wasted, as Wolfe was
the first to admit; in his too-muchness he wrote "millions of
words in the course of shaping out and defining a volume of a
few hundred thousand." But finally a manuscript was completed and, according to the legend, Wolfe characteristically
signalized the occasion of the book's going off to the printer by
feasting on an eight-pound steak.

Though *Of Time and the River* does not have the unity of
Look Homeward, Angel, it is the most typically Wolfean of the

four major novels, for it has all the qualities popularly associated with its author. Poetry is still abundantly present, a youth still looks with wonder and pain and elation as he seeks fulfillment in the world, the novel is pleasantly diffuse, and it is long (912 pages).

In a general way, *Of Time and the River* matches Wolfe's life from 1920 to 1925. Story-line is bare. The opening page picks up Eugene the day after his conversation with Ben's ghost in the last chapter of *Look Homeward, Angel*. With his family around him, Eugene is awaiting a train to go north. He attends Harvard as a graduate student, returns home briefly before going to New York, teaches at a metropolitan university, visits a wealthy friend at a Hudson River estate, goes to Europe, and on the voyage back meets a woman who is to have a great influence on his life. These are the events of the book. Properly *Of Time and the River* has been called a "novel on wheels."

While there is no suspense or plot-involvement in the ordinary literary sense, the book is constructed on a deliberate plan. Wolfe wished, as the subtitle indicates, to write "A Legend of Man's Hunger in His Youth." Beneath the subtitle he cited Ecclesiastes 3:21, "Who knoweth the spirit of man that goeth upward, and the spirit of the beast that goeth downward to the earth?"—calling attention to the godlike nature of the sublime quest. After the moving dedication to his "dauntless and unshaken friend" Perkins, Wolfe invoked Plato with a quotation from the *Crito,* in which Socrates, in order to be ruled by the mystic voices of justice and truth, turned aside all arguments that he save himself from disgrace and death. These mottoes are concluded with the poem (in German) opening Book III of Goethe's *Wilhelm Meister's Apprenticeship,* "Kennst du das Land, wo die Zitronen blühn" (Know you the land where the citron-apples bloom), expressing youth's yearning for romance and ending with an invitation to one's father to accompany him. The mood is thus set for a young man's courageous search.

The Story of a Novel contains Wolfe's frequently quoted

statement that "the deepest search in life . . . that in one way or another was central to all living was man's search to find a father, not merely the father of his flesh, not merely the lost father of his youth, but the image of a strength and wisdom external to his need and superior to his hunger, to which the belief and power of his own life could be united." This Joycean idea was Perkins' offhand suggestion to Wolfe, who received it enthusiastically, and clearly Wolfe intended it to infuse the pages of *Of Time and the River*. Eugene's adventures are those of a youth trying to find a mooring for his trusts and beliefs. The image has genuine force. In practically all fiction, a human being is looking for that which he does not have. Eugene lacked a knowledge of life's meaning. If he could find the Father, the understanding might be his; and so Eugene (and Wolfe, through an act of creation) sifted his experiences to see whether he might not come upon a solution of the puzzle.

From the first outline of the book, initially titled "The October Fair," Wolfe decided to give shape to Eugene's search by the use of certain Greek legends which would almost never be mentioned except in the eight section headings. From time to time, the hero would be Orestes, Telemachus, Proteus, Jason, Antaeus, and Kronos; twice, departing from the Greek myths, he would be Faust. Each would suggest the nature of the journey in that particular segment.

Before embarking on the Orestean course, Wolfe affixed a prose-poem in which with Biblical cadences he repeated some of the symbols of *Look Homeward, Angel* and then spoke of the search for the Father. The main emphasis, however, was on the endurance of the earth in contrast to the passing and death of the flesh. Only immortal love endured as the earth endured. From these poetic paragraphs the phrase most echoed throughout the novel is ". . . of wandering forever and the earth again. . ." By "earth again" Wolfe explained that he meant simply "a place for the heart to come to," but according to Virginia Stevens there is more to the phrase than that. The "wandering" is equivalent to the North, to the Father, and to the

74

eternal seeking; the "earth" is the South, the mother, the need for roots. These opposites were combined in Eugene, and from their unresolved contradistinction the events of the narrative develop.

Perhaps the variety of *Of Time and the River* can best be disclosed by defining each of the eight sections in turn.

❧

BOOK I. ORESTES: FLIGHT BEFORE FURY. It was afternoon, and as Eugene's family stood on a railway platform in the mountains of Old Catawba in the South, they chatted back and forth with the good humor and banter of those who felt close to each other because of their blood-ties. Eugene was eager to get away from the entangling web of his family. He boarded the train and moved northward across Old Catawba, his excitement indicated by a hymn to fury: "Who has seen fury riding in the mountains?" The word *fury* can here be translated as the restlessness of a young man. In the Pullman smoker he met some Babbitt-like men talking of politics and real estate. Wolfe represents them far more subtly than Sinclair Lewis does with the same type of characters in "The Man Who Knew Coolidge" (1928). Eugene knew at that very moment that similar talk was going on in Pullman cars all over America. Later, he got drunk with Robert Weaver, a society-conscious Altamont fellow his own age, and the scene is followed by a jazzy poem of drunkenness. These inebriated pages embody wild moonlight prose, nonsense Latin, and impassioned cadenzas on America, then finally move into dithyrambs: "The moon slept over the mountains and lay like silence in the desert, and it carved the shadows of great rocks like time."

In the morning the boy visited his father in a great hospital and grieved that the powerful man, sucked of life by the cancer, was now dead in every essential except the "great hands of the stonecutter," symbols of the deathlessness of the creative. Throughout this twenty-four-hour episode Eugene was driven on, like Orestes, "as helpless as a leaf upon a hurricane."

75

The account is interlarded with frequent interruptions by Time. As the train came in, the group on the platform were "fixed" in Time, only the train moving. Then in the Pullman car Ben was mentioned by one of the men, and the present moment was blotted out, and Eugene was back to the hour on his twelfth birthday when Ben gave him a watch. The Pullman car was obliterated, and only after the refrain "Up on the mountain, down in the valley, deep, deep, in the hill, Ben— cold, cold, cold," did the faces and voices in the Pullman swing back into place. Shortly afterwards, upon an inquiry concerning his father, memory hurled Eugene back to early reminiscences of the stonecutter.

This Orestes section, with its driving motion, is the first of Wolfe's many incantations on America. By means of a journey by train, one could in less than a day go seven hundred miles across the land, participate momentarily in thousands of lives, and "see pass before his eyes the infinite panorama of shifting images that make a nation's history." Eugene's hunger for contact was "the furious hunger that so haunts and hurts Americans" everywhere. Like others, he would hurl himself down the landscape, looking restlessly for the door behind which to hide his nakedness and find his home. Eugene could never forget the sight of the little towns at night as seen from the train, itself the "rhythm of suspended time, the sound of silence and forever." There in the villages alongside the railroad tracks he got a brief vision of the lights blinking, the stores and houses, but no life anywhere, no door. All was in "frozen cataleptic silence." The loneliness and hugeness of America, on which Wolfe was later to expand, is here accentuated by the quick forward rush of a train in darkness.

BOOK II. YOUNG FAUSTUS. When Eugene, the Faustian student-philosopher seeking all knowledge, arrived at Harvard, his hunger to know everything and have everything and be everything reached toward fanaticism. Besides the often physical hunger of the body, there was the hunger for books and the hunger for people. At the college library he assaulted the shelves as though, by reading all the pages in the books, he could somehow be satisfied. "He pictured himself as tearing the entrails from a book as from a fowl." When the devouring of books did not satiate, he kept charts of the miles he had traveled, the people he had known, the women he had slept with. He kept other charts of what he planned to do, far beyond the energies of any thousand men. At other times, he roamed the streets of Cambridge and Boston and "became a kind of gigantic eavesdropper upon life." He felt that he wanted to know the lives of fifty million people, visit every country, learn a hundred languages, possess ten thousand women and yet "have one he loved and honored above all." At a restaurant on Tremont Street he ate countless times because of a waitress there whom he never even spoke to with any familiarity. He merely watched her and itched to know every trifle of her life. But usually, once Eugene met people, he squeezed them dry of any warmth, then with boredom turned away from them. There were, after all, millions of others from whom he had much to learn. When in his frenzy, he wanted to consume not only books and people but all the earth, and was downcast when he realized he could not do it. Still the Faustian longing did not wane.

Of Eugene's studies at the university, little is told except for Professor Hatcher's class in playwriting, where he compensated for a feeling of social inferiority by boasting of his superior difference. To him, the other students were empty sophisticates trying to escape life, and their work evinced this truth in well-made anemic plays or plagiarisms from Chekhov or the German Expressionists. Unlike the earthy Eugene, none of them were artists, nor did they have "the first, the last, the foremost quality of the artist, without which he is lost: the ability to get out of his own life the power to live and work by, to derive from his own experience—as a fruit of all his seeing, feeling, joy and bitter anguish—the palpable and living substance of his art." Among his acquaintances at the univer-

77

sity Eugene had, except for Professor Hatcher, but one real friend.

This was Francis Starwick, Hatcher's assistant. Though he was from the raw Midwest, Starwick had found a niche for himself among the Harvard esthetes. Like Eugene, he wanted to tell the story of America, structured on the image of the mighty Mississippi River which he knew well from having lived near it. But though he had the artist's spirit, he had not the fiber for the job, and eventually he relinquished his ambition to Eugene. Starwick's hold on the unpolished Eugene came from a "rare and priceless quality that is seldom found in any one, and almost never in Americans, of being able to give to any simple act a glamour of luxury, pleasure, excitement." In his presence everything assumed a brightness and opulence which it had never before had. Eugene worshiped him, though he was aware that Starwick lacked "that one small grain of common earth" which would give him life. Starwick was the first of many people in Eugene's adventures to permit him a glimpse of the enchanting world of art and sophistication he so longed for.

During his years at Harvard, Eugene was drawn into the family circle of Uncle Bascom Pentland, his mother's brother, a tall, mad, mountain man, in his lustiness and vigor a strong contrast to the fragile, effeminate Starwick. Though once a preacher of various denominations, he was now a lawyer in the city, and at his office there and at his home in the suburbs Eugene often visited him. The boy, from listening to Uncle Bascom's experiences, launched vicariously into the past, and saw there the shapes of sturdy Americans.

Also pitted against the artificiality of Starwick and the Harvard playwrights was W. O. Gant, the description of whose death is said by Pamela Hansford Johnson to be "comparable for power and pity and horror with the death of Ben" in *Look Homeward, Angel*. Only two other death scenes, she says, one from Martin du Gard and one from Proust, stand with it. The night before cancer of the prostate finally drained the far wanderer of life, Gant went back in memory, Wolfe writes, to his Pennsylvania boyhood; memories crowded upon memories; and then Gant made his peace with Eliza. In his last moments he was a child again, he was redeemed, he found his way. When Eugene arrived for the funeral (these chapters are told from the point of view of Helen), the boy was once more haunted by Gant's hands, which lived on. Death might destroy the body, but creativity was indestructible.

Eugene went back to his studies at Harvard, had his final conversation with the tragic Starwick, and the section ends.

In "Young Faustus" Eugene's continuing exploration of America was advanced as a result of his initial contact with an alien society in a metropolitan area. More than before, he was convinced not only of the variety of American life but of its loneliness. His intimacy with the middling Simpson family with all their "folly, falseness, and hypocrisy," huddling themselves together for protection against the wreckage America imposed on those who dwelt in it, convinced him too of its terror.

Book III. Telemachus. When Ulysses failed to return from the Trojan war, his son Telemachus set out to look for him. In this section of the novel, Wolfe was thinking, too, of Stephen Dedalus, Joyce's young artist.

The action takes up Eugene in the autumn after his years at Cambridge. He had come back to Altamont to await the acceptance of a play he had written and submitted to a New York producer. The interlude provided a period of meditation. Time was always moving away from him. It was his enemy. He could not seem to recapture the past, yet it was almost death to lose it. In a great paean to October, a month when all things returned, Eugene's thoughts were filled with his lost Father, with Time, and with the flowing River. All of them were one and the same. Perhaps in October, his Father would return. With his mother, Eliza, the boy talked long, realizing "her invincible strength, hope, and fortitude and her will that was more strong than death, her character that was as solid as a rock." Then came word about the play: "We regret." The youth felt that his family, in discouraging his ambitions to be a dramatist, were right after all. He was defeated.

In a mood of dejection, Eugene went on a drunken ride down the mountain with Robert Weaver and two other friends. In a small town in South Carolina they were arrested and thrown into jail by several brutal policemen. After his release, Eugene decided he had to prove to Eliza that her faith, now all that was left to him, was justified. To do so, he had to get away; he heard the "great train" in the night. He had not found his Father, and still Time passed.

"Telemachus" is a melancholy interlude inserted among Eugene's experiences away from home. It is Wolfe's poem on the theme of returning.

Book IV. Proteus: The City. Proteus, the son of Poseidon (Neptune), was able to assume a hundred different shapes at will. So it was with the city of New York and its many faces. Eugene's New York sojourn takes up but half this section, the last hundred pages moving him up the River on a visit to a wealthy family. Of his stay in the city, three portions are well defined, all having to do with his teaching at a university.

First, in order to pursue his playwriting, Eugene accepted an instructorship of English in a metropolitan college at $1800 a year. The move was unsatisfactory on many scores. Though he spent little time in the classroom buildings, he noted with distaste the violent jealousy among his fellow instructors as they jockeyed for position and promotion. He was annoyed that the grading of freshman themes shucked him of time and energy to write his plays, and he was constantly revolted by the stupidity of his students. In these passages Wolfe resorts to some disquieting but highly readable caricature.

As a second emphasis, Wolfe has the story of Abe Jones, a typical, overly persistent Jewish student who "fed on Eugene's life." The more Eugene gave, the more Abe wanted. Abe blocked his exit from the classroom, followed him down the street, asked him insulting questions. Why were the theme top-

THOMAS CLAYTON WOLFE
ASHEVILLE, N. C.
Age, 19; Weight, 178; Height, 6 feet 3 inches

Di Society; Buncombe County Club; Freshman-Sophomore Debate (2); Dramatic Association; Carolina Playmakers (3, 4); Author two One-Act Plays, Executive Committee (4); Associate Editor YACKETY YACK (3); Associate Editor *Magazine* (3); Assistant Editor-in-Chief (4); Managing Editor *Tar Heel* (3); Editor-in-Chief (4); Advisory Board *Tar Baby* (4); Worth Prize in Philosophy (3); Y. M. C. A. Cabinet (3, 4); Student Council (4); Athletic Council (4); Class Poet (3, 4); Chairman Junior Stunt Committee; German Club; Amphoterothen; Satyrs; Golden Fleece.

Σ Υ; Ω Δ; Π Κ Φ.

EDITING the *Tar Heel*, winning Horace's philosophy prize when only a Junior, writing plays and then showing the world how they should be acted—they are all alike to this young Shakespeare. Last year he played the leading role in the "Midnight Frolic" at "Gooch's Winter Palace", but this year it's the leading role on the "Carolina Shipping Board". But, seriously speaking, "Buck" is a great, big fellow. He can do more between 8:25 and 8:30 than the rest of us can do all day, and it is no wonder that he is classed as a genius.

University of North Carolina Annual, 1920

81

ics not better? Why not a more suitable textbook? Why were
there no Jewish writers on the reading list? In short, why did
Eugene not do everything differently from the way he did do
it? Eugene felt cornered and undone. Yet in the long run
Eugene realized that Abe was his friend—and a symbol of
the city—trying, not unlike himself, to find the door.

Last are the pages on Eugene's residence at the Hotel Leopold and his acid comments on the old, retired, lifeless guests
who stayed there, notably a woman who had once been a pros-
perous abortionist but who now went about spouting clichés
from the great moral poets.

A memorable episode in *Of Time and the River* is Eugene's
visit to Joel Pierce at Far Field Farm over a Fourth of July
week end. It illustrates Wolfe's practice of combining a number of incidents into a single section of a book; for Wolfe went
many times to stay with his friend Olin Dows on his family's
estate up the Hudson. Here all Wolfe's trips there are compacted into one visit for Eugene.

Eugene arrived at Far Field Farm on a moonlight evening
when the lush landscape was washed in silver, anesthetizing
him into a romantic mood. Joel's family, cultured and out-
wardly friendly, had no knowledge of New York Jews or Irish-
men and were puzzled when Eugene spoke in admiration of
them. Mrs. Pierce believed that Art was hardly more than
screen-painting. On a nearby estate Eugene was participant in
a holiday celebration with fireworks and outdoor motion pic-
tures for the families of wealth and prominence. In his "moonlight" mood Eugene did not recall the cost in human effort
and despair it took to build these palaces. He was too fasci-
nated by the vast icebox, the enormous kitchen, the beautiful
leathered library. Eugene read his play "Mannerhouse" to
Joel and his sister, both of whom praised it.

Not till Eugene's encounter with Joel's mannered and im-
perious grandfather was his enchantment dispelled. The grand
old man thought anyone a "cad" who would put personal
knowledge of others into print (Eugene had only that morning

admitted such use in his "Mannerhouse"), and it made no difference to the strongly opinionated old fellow if it was Rousseau, Byron, Musset, or George Sand. Eugene was shocked that one could, presuming upon the privilege of wealth, assume such unconsidered judgment of genius, and more shocked still when the mild, kindly Joel would not allow his grandfather to see him in the summer comfort of shirt sleeves. The distance between Eugene and the great folk of Far Field Farm was wide, the moonlight rapture was gone, and the boy realized that America, so beautiful especially at such luxurious places as the Farm, lay nevertheless in the hungry and the searching and the living, and not in the moon-enchanted. America was still fierce and savage. In the face of his hurt sense of class distinctions he was glad to board the train and note the multifariousness of human kind in the cars. He went down the River which bore "him on forever out of magic to all the grime and sweat and violence of the city, the unceasing city, the million-footed city, and into America." The door had opened briefly and closed again.

Connecting the university portion of Book IV with the portion about Far Field Farm is a remarkable prose poem in which there is a recapitulation and blending of themes and symbols, with new ones introduced, but all applicable to the city and America. The city was a "protean and phantasmal shape of time." It was a

> Proud, cruel, everchanging and ephemeral city, to whom we came once when our hearts were high, our blood passionate and hot, our brain a particle of fire: infinite and mutable city, mercurial city, strange citadel of million-visaged time—Oh! endless river and eternal rock, in which the forms of life came, passed and changed intolerably before us, and to which we came, as every youth has come, with such enormous madness, and with so mad a hope—for what?

In the city a young man, as Eugene noted earlier, wasted his youth, but since it was an inevitable misspending, there was no help for it. The city gave to Eugene neither his Father nor his America.

Book V. Jason's Voyage. In the myth, Jason (Eugene) set out over the sea for distant Colchis (Europe) to recapture the Golden Fleece (the lost Father) in order that he might return and claim his father's throne (America). "Here was the great boy Jason," Wolfe had written of Eugene before the overseas journey began, "looking for brothers in the fellowship of that inspired adventure of man's youth—the proud, deathless image of what all of us desire when young, where was it?"

The first stop on the pilgrimage was Oxford, where Eugene lived for a while with the Coulson family. Unlike Americans in their wilderness, most of the English, Eugene perceived, had found "a way, a door, a room to enter." The Coulsons, though, were different; they were lost in the fog of England. The daughter Edith envied Eugene's coming from "a young country— where nothing that you did yesterday matters very much." She believed that Americans were indeed fortunate. Even more distressing than the Coulson family were the Rhodes scholars from America, deadened by an inferiority feeling, clinging together desperately before the "door they could not open."

Eugene moved over to Paris, and on New Year's Eve unexpectedly met Starwick on the steps of the Louvre and later was introduced to a pair of Boston women who were Starwick's friends. Elinor (Mrs. Marjorie C. Fairbanks), thirty years old, had followed Starwick to Paris, leaving her husband and child behind. The other was Ann, perfect example of the big, dark, beautiful, serious New Englander. By now, Starwick was effete, entirely continental.

In this group Eugene felt like a country bumpkin; but for two months he launched with them into a "world of night and Paris and debauch." Eugene knew that Starwick's ambition was gone, and he was sickened by the man's sophisticated sentimentality about Europeans, inferring that Americans like himself could never possess either delicacy or nobility. Despite Eugene's realization that both the women were emotionally

attached to Starwick, Eugene fell in love with Ann, who rejected him completely and at once. Starwick, meanwhile, pre-
cipitated several disgraceful drunken scenes and kept at his
side a French youth for whom he acknowledged devotion. The
gradual revelation of Starwick's perversion was brought to a
head when Eugene struck his friend in resentment and anger.
After a final night of festivity, the antic players separated.

Eugene's comical pursuit of Ann—*comical* as Wolfe relates it
—has two solemn implications, one looking backward and one
forward. During that final ridiculous scene with her at the
country pension, Eugene redefined "the buried life, the funda-
mental structure of the great family of earth to which all men
belong." The revival of this mood from his boyhood in Old
Catawba overjoyed him. The second was the notion on which
Wolfe was later to elaborate more fully: in some way Ann
made "palpable the female quality" of America. For Wolfe,
then, it was as a woman that the ideal of America took shape
in dreams, and so it was as Eugene looked upon Ann.

One section of "Jason's Voyage" has caused unnecessary confusion: the twenty pages from Eugene's notebook, written in
the first person. Robert Penn Warren, for instance, accused
Wolfe of writing indifferently "Eugene Gant" or "I." It is a
matter of record that Wolfe wrote *Of Time and the River* in
the first person, and the switch to third was made by John Hall
Wheelock of Scribners. The notebook section, apparently
printed verbatim from Wolfe's Paris diary, was unchanged.
Respectable precedent for the interpolated diary can be found
in the closing chapters of Joyce's *A Portrait of the Artist as
a Young Man*. At any rate, the notebook provides the reader
with a naked view of what both Eugene Gant and Thomas
Wolfe were thinking at this period. There are literary opinions,
comments on art, ideas jotted down as in all writers' notebooks,
patriotic arguments such as that the American novelist Harold
Bell Wright was superior to pumped-up foreigners like Henri
Bordeaux, conclusions such as that "More and more I am convinced that to be a great writer a man must be something of an

ass," and also serious reflections about the role of the American artist who, unlike the European, must forego ease and grace in order to deal with a sprawling country and "its hundred million tongues, its unfound form, its unborn art." More than any-where else in the long novel, Wolfe made clear in these pages the impossibility of the task which he was trying to per-form.

BOOK VI. ANTÆUS: EARTH AGAIN. The son of Poseidon (Neptune) and the Earth goddess Gaea, Antaeus searched for his father whom he had never seen. He was invulnerable in any contest, for he continually gained strength from contact with his mother earth. Defeat came only when Hercules held him in the air and strangled him.

Eugene sensed the renewal of his strength when, leaving the trio in Paris, he took a train away from the city and back to the country. All the way down to Orléans, he revived with the rain-washed landscape and the earthy passengers along the route. "Le soleil . . . la pluie . . . la terre," he chanted. In the provincial capital he met a busy little comtesse who insisted on believing he was a journalist for the *New York Times* who would publicize the need of money for a hospital sponsored by herself and a grandiose marquise. Before he could extricate him-self from this "web of absurd circumstance," he realized "the aimless lack of purpose in his wandering" and set his course straight again.

BOOK VII. KRONOS AND RHEA: THE DREAM OF TIME. This is the second of the three short concluding parts of the novel. In the myth, Rhea, an earth goddess like her mother Gaea, helped her children against their father Kronos, who gobbled them up as soon as they were born to prevent their overthrow-ing him. Yet Wolfe seems not to have this part of the legend in mind. He writes that he called the section " 'Cronos and Rhea' (or perhaps simply 'Time and the River'—that means 'Memory and Change')." The Greek word for *time* is *chrono;* the suffix *–rrhea* means *flow*. By the end of the section, Eugene is suf-fused with evidence of his Father but, like Antaeus, he has not seen him. Perhaps Wolfe meant that Memory and Change had made it possible for the search to be terminated, especially now that love was soon to be born.

There is little action in "Kronos and Rhea," yet it is one of the essential episodes in Eugene's adventures. From Orléans he went over to Tours, "a place of quietness and pause," and there all day, all night, his thoughts turned upon home. And then he began to write. Visions came, and dreams, visions of delight and joy, of guilt and ruin. They became surrealistic, yet he kept them under control. He began to live in the past, actually to *live*, which was different from living in imagination. One day, in this Dream of Time and Memory, he found he was penniless. Back in Orléans, the Comtesse de Caux gave him fare to Paris. From there he went on to Marseilles, got a glimpse of Starwick and the two women, but fled. He had an "evil dream," almost indistinguishable from insanity, and finally he lost the time-sense entirely, not knowing what he did nor where he was. In Dijon the sound of a church bell brought back remembrance of the college bell at Pulpit Hill. The noises in the Dijon square took him away fifteen years to his youth in Altamont—"and he was closer to his childhood and his father's life of power and magnificence than he could ever be again in savage America." He began to try to define the essence of Americans. "He thought of home." He wished to recapture time (like Proust), to arrest it, and then to "fix" it, as a critic has explained, "in the eternity of fiction." Had Eugene found the Father? Whether or no, the search was over.

BOOK VIII. FAUST AND HELEN. The medieval Faust wanted, more than anything else, to find his Helen; and on an ocean liner headed toward America, Eugene saw a Helen who was both beautiful and knowledgeable. "Esther was fair; she was fair; she had dove's eyes." Eugene was in love now, and not as before.

So does *Of Time and the River* end, briefly, with a promise.

ᦦ ᦧ

The amplification here given the eight separate parts of *Of Time and the River* obviates a general examination of the novel. Only a few matters need re-emphasis.

In the title, the intended fluidity of the narrative is forecast. There is, always, a moving forward. *The Story of a Novel* reveals that three kinds of Time are operative in Eugene's adventures: present time, which merely advances the story; past time, which more or less in its accumulation governs character and event; and immutable time, which to Wolfe was the time of rivers, mountains, earth, and oceans. A fixity of time is possible only through Art.

The time element is balanced by a space element: the river. Like time, the river never stops and, like time, it has a permanent, unchanging quality. Both time and river epitomize the typical wanderers of the American continent. Over and over the notion finds expression. A particularly apt incident is the one when Eugene watches the crowds in Boston's South Station, the great trains—symbols also of flow—emptying and loading people; and "all was as it had always been, moving, changing, swarming on forever like a river, and as fixed, unutterable in unceasing movement and in changeless change as the great river is, and time itself." The whole paradox implicit in time and space permeates Eugene's story.

The search for the Father, the principal image of course, proceeds through this maze. There is an exit only where creativity begins—as happened during Eugene's dream at Tours.

Not always are Wolfe's symbols so clear. Like the ghost in *Look Homeward, Angel,* they fade from one identity into another and then coincide. Often, though seemingly different, the Father-search becomes synonymous with the America which Wolfe is trying to define. His ancestors, it occurred to Eugene, "were great men and knew the wilderness" and, by sowing "their blood and sperm across the continent," had formed it. They were America, elusive to Eugene, though he was "his father's son, shaped from his father's earth of blood and sweat and toil and bitter agony." As Orestes, he set out;

and as Young Faustus he was constantly aware of her (America, his Father), yet he kept looking for her. At moments, in poetry, he caught up with her; at others, in thought, she was a fable: "It is a fabulous country, the only fabulous country; it is the one place where miracles not only happen, but where they happen all the time." She was not in the city among the "young pavement lives," nor among the wealthy at Far Field Farm, but there somewhere on the continent—a single substance and a million patterns. She was not in Europe. Yet, oddest of oddities, there he made the first step in his rediscovery of her. He wrote in his *Letters:* "I could not sleep for thinking of the sights and sounds and colors, the whole intolerable memory of America, its violence, savagery, immensity, beauty, ugliness, and glory." The discovery of America was there where Ben told him the world was: within himself.

This first step, to be succeeded by a glimpse of his dark Helen, gave Wolfe the impetus to continue the quest with more definiteness than that characterized by the emotional disruptions which formerly dissipated his progress.

✒️ ✑

Aside from the ideas underlying *Of Time and the River,* there is the matter of style and method. Though Wolfe has now been rather forgiven, many early readers objected to his poetic flights, which they considered were outside the novelist's province. Others were annoyed by his caricature, one of Wolfe's strongest literary devices. And still others objected to his exposure of the Cambridge playwrights, the students and instructors at the metropolitan university, all of whom are stripped of pretenses by Wolfe's satire. He did not despise them; he simply looked inside. Occasionally he resorted to sarcasm: for instance, about the pale Harvard esthetes at Miss Potter's party, who revealed themselves as despicable amateurs, freaks, poisoned misfits, denuded of life and vitality. At times Wolfe could be overly harsh, as he generally was with those he considered the breathing dead.

89

Thomas Wolfe

Wolfe had a keen ear for dialect, which he often used to sharpen the satire. The Boston Irish, the New York Jews, the Far Field Farm people, the French, and other defined groups speak in transcriptions of both phrasing and dialectical spelling. Listen to an Englishman: "Did you ever read—that is, in recent yöhs—the concluding chaptahs in 'The Vicah of Wakefield'? . . . I was reading it just the other day. It's an . . . *'strawd'n'ry'* thing!"

Even when Wolfe's satire was understood and his wild poetry approved, critical readers objected to a style often jammed with marching nouns and adjectives. Such a passage was this:

> somewhere across the illimitable fields and folds and woods and hills and hollows of America, across the huge brown earth, the mown fields, the vast wild space, the lavish, rude and unfenced distances, the familiar, homely, barren, harsh, strangely haunting scenery of the nation . . .

Such a style, they said, indicated a lack of discipline, as did the novel itself. But this very headlong, desperate fullness is a facet of Wolfe's difference. A pruned style and a formalized structure were no more his concern than they were Walt Whitman's. Without his ways, he would have been another writer entirely, minus richness and sensuousness and abundance.

In his notebook Eugene wrote: "I must think. I must mix it all with myself and with America." As he did this, he discovered he could not shut himself behind the wall he had begun to build in *Look Homeward, Angel*. He could not do it as hero or as artist or as a human being. America was much too vast; no man could build a wall so high. The provincial from the hill country, out upon the world, had learned the second lesson in his education.

5

~§ "THE WEB AND THE ROCK"

Wolfe did not carry Eugene nearly so far in *Of Time and the River* as he had intended. For the book he had written a long love story which would come just after Eugene's return to America and then extend several hundred pages. But publishing limitations prevented that, and Eugene was allowed to meet the lady only in the last chapter. At that point the reader learns that her name was Esther. The narrative of the whole affair was postponed till the publication of the third novel. Wolfe was not necessarily discouraged. There were many books in him, he knew, and the love story would eventually be used.

The critical reaction to *Of Time and the River,* however, considerably altered this plan. Angered by insistent accusations that he was capable of nothing but lyrical autobiography, Wolfe decided that he would show *them*—whoever *they* were—that he could be as inventive as any other writer. And he would go to any lengths to prove it. There were, in addition, other considerations operating in his mind. Apparently he also wished to relieve his family of further distress on account of his portraits of them. And—a vital matter—he had certain Asheville material from his boyhood not yet in a book. A full change of course was indicated. First of all, he did away with Eugene Gant. In his place arose Monk Webber. The Gant family disappeared, replaced by the Joyners. Wolfe switched publishers from Scribners to Harpers. He switched editors. The change was complete —or so he thought.

In May, 1938, when he turned over his pile of manuscript to Edward Aswell before going West, he prepared an Author's Note about his third novel: "This novel, then, marks not only a turning away from the books I have written in the past, but a genuine spiritual and artistic change. It is the most objective novel that I have written." While no one can deny Wolfe's sincerity in this statement, the fact remains that the "change" he spoke of was not much of a change at all. True, his hero had been born in a new town. But Libya Hill, except in name, was Altamont—or Asheville, if you will. Monk Webber was Eugene Gant—or Thomas Wolfe, if you will. The Joyners were just other members of the Gant-Wolfe family. And Esther, when she came on the scene later, was still the first Esther with only a last name added.

The love story which concludes *Of Time and the River* takes up again on page 297 of *The Web and Rock*. Clearly, from that point on, Wolfe's revision of the manuscript was confined principally to substituting the physical Monk for the physical Eugene. He also rewrote a few passages to show that Monk was mostly at fault for his treatment of Esther. Unmodified was the spirit of the hero.

Yet, even if we dismiss these strange circumstances as unimportant, *The Web and the Rock* is a disappointing effort. It is generally considered the least attractive of Wolfe's four novels, and some of Wolfe's most devoted admirers have found it distressingly uneven as well as annoying. As we know, his method of writing was to complete an episode here, an episode there, as the mood struck him. The transitions and fillers came later. But Wolfe did not live to provide the connections, nor to iron out the discrepancies. The galley proofs—an essential element in the Wolfe workshop—he never saw. Edward Aswell tells how, to provide continuity for the various sections of the two novels published after Wolfe's death, he "wrote a few paragraphs as best I could to serve this purpose, drawing upon Tom's own words whenever they were available, and these passages were printed in italics and set on pages by themselves in order to distinguish them from Tom's own text." If all in all Aswell served Wolfe very well indeed, *The Web and the Rock* must yet be discussed on the basis of that which is before us.

What Wolfe intended doing in the novel was bluntly stated in his Author's Note. The book was to reveal "one man's discovery of life and of the world . . . discovery through a process of finding out . . . through being mistaken and wrong and an idiot and egotistical and aspiring and hopeful and believing and confused, and pretty much what every one of us is, and goes through, and finds out about, and becomes." In short, it was to be what the first two novels were, the story of "the sensitive young fellow in conflict with his town, his family, the little world around him . . . the whole adventure of apprenticeship and discovery."

Such a task, Wolfe believed, was a tremendous assignment, though he was willing to assay it; and in the prose-poem prefacing the first section and beginning "Could I make tongue say more than tongue could utter!" he cried out that if he could write words as great as his hunger, he would be satisfied, for then he should have "beaten death."

As Wolfe composed his hero's new background and as he revised the portions concerned with the love affair, he valiantly tried to invent a style which would be more objective and less lyrical than his customary one. Though it was not in him to pass up the poetry entirely, he partially succeeded, especially in the first half of the book. By the time Monk meets Esther Jack, however, the dithyrambs return with their lilting sentences and familiar images. The leaf, the river, and Time are evoked in

93

their usual context to give color and meaning to Monk's experiences, as they did to Eugene's.

Two other images are now emphasized. In *Of Time and the River,* Boston was an "ancient web," into which the million-footed man-swarm passed. In *The Web and the Rock* the web is, first, the tangle of Joyner inheritance from which Monk cannot escape. Later it is, more gently, "the whole dense weft and web of plain humanity everywhere that weave the homely threads of this great earth together." Finally it seems to Monk that Esther and he have somehow "spun together" a web in which he is trapped. Like the ghost in *Look Homeward, Angel,* the image twists, but always it is the mesh keeping man from freedom and individuality and himself.

The *rock* has no connection with the *stone* of the earlier books. It is, specifically, the city of New York—"that enfabled rock," Wolfe wrote, "that ship of life, that swarming, million-footed, tower-masted, and sky-roaring citadel that bears the magic name of the Island of Manhattan." It is the fabulous dream-place for which all young men yearn. When Monk is most in love with Esther, the city appears to be "carved out of a single rock, shaped to a single pattern, moving forever to a single harmony, a central, all-inclusive energy." Then, in contrast to the ever moving Hudson, the rock is Esther with "dark time . . . flowing by her like a river." In the final pages the reader may agree with Alfred Kazin that the rock represents "the waste and chagrin of experience."

Within the quicksilver fluctuations of these two symbols, the story of Monk Webber proceeds.

⋅⋅§ ⋅§⋅

Like his alter ego Eugene Gant, George Webber was born in 1900 in a mountain town of the South. His father John Webber, who had come as a contractor in 1881 from Pennsylvania to Old Catawba, married a local girl Amelia Joyner about 1885. When their one child was eight years old, John decamped with another man's wife; and on Amelia's death, George was reared by his Aunt Maw Joyner, spinster of seventy. As the boy grew up, he developed thin legs, long arms, big hands, and a pair of heavy shoulders supporting a large head which protruded forward with deep-set eyes and a low forehead—hence the nickname Monk.

The Joyner mountain clan lived in "dateless Joyner time." Their "weblike" memories fed on tales of superstition and death. The Civil War was only yesterday. Their roots were of the lonely frontier, but sure. Yet when Monk daydreamed, it was never of his mother's proud but almost illiterate people, but of his father's life and land—the far-off golden city, the promise of a distant America. To him, these two worlds were a "tangled web" which "touched but never joined."

As Wolfe tells the story of Monk's first sixteen years, he gives little space to recording Monk's development as a well-defined character. There is no mention, for instance, of his going to school, and only bare accounts of his *doing* anything at all. The narrative advances on three other planes. First, much is told about such boyhood companions as Randy Shepperton and the heroic Nebraska Crane and the "fat and priestly" Jerry Alsop, all of whom are to have a role in Monk's biography later on. Second, there are numerous essays on various aspects of Libya Hill and Old Catawba, on the hour of Three O'Clock, on the connotation of proper names, on bad boys and bad parts of town, on Pity, on Beauty; but these essays seem hardly the thoughts of a boy of twelve or so. Third, Wolfe provides a generous supply of tragic episodes in almost all of which Monk is nonparticipant. In these, killings and accidents are plentiful. Captain Suggs was a cripple, Baxter Lampley a thief.

The most famous of the digressions is "The Child by Tiger," in which the religious Negro houseman, Dick Prosser, went amuck one wintry evening and murdered those who blocked his path. This expert tale is compounded on Dick's good-and-evil nature, accentuated by black and white contrasts, the snow and the night, the light and the dark. As Dick's life was molded by "those powers discrete that wage perpetual warfare in the

Student Wolfe, spring 1920   *University of North Carolina Library*

lives of all men living," so was George Webber's dual nature split between the worlds of his father and his mother.

These anecdotes of street and town and people, enchanting and haunting as most of them are, remain static events in relationship to the personality presumably evolving within Monk. As we know, they are, in the main, unused reminiscences from Wolfe's childhood.

When John Webber died in 1916, he left George a small inheritance on which the boy drew to pay his expenses at Pine Rock College, a small backwoods Baptist institution. Already on the campus was Jerry Alsop, mothering a group of innocent youngsters into an acceptance of the false purity and the high-sounding but hollow idealism characteristic of the 1910's. Monk was a rebel from this group, especially after their condemnation of his admiration for *Crime and Punishment,* unfortunately not on their approved list of books by Dickens and others. Rather, Monk admired Jim Randolph (William Folger), football hero and man of the world; and the most memorable event of Monk's college years was his going to Richmond for a football game in which Randolph starred.

This portion of the novel, unlike Eugene Gant's sojourn at Pulpit Hill, is short. Wolfe's principal intention is to stress the wide gap between the empty character-building philosophy of the red-brick college, and the shocking reality of its provincialism and narrowness.

After graduation Monk went to New York; and no American author can write so ebulliently about a young man's first encounter with the city as can Thomas Wolfe. The intoxication, the glory, the promise are all there. The city was the symbol of a man's hope; it was what a man had "within his heart." And in the city, Monk believed that now he had his father's heritage, even though the Joyner web had not been torn away.

For a while Monk and several other stripling Southerners shared an apartment with Jim Randolph on 123rd Street. Jim brought excitement into the apartment, and there were parties and girls. But gradually Monk began to realize that the older

97

and more mature Jim could not bear to think of himself as past his youth and that he fed on the life of his younger companions. Monk moved to a room on Fourteenth Street and lived alone.

Wolfe does not make clear just what it was Monk was doing in New York. He had no job. Then suddenly and without preliminaries we are told that Webber "had grown sick and weary in his heart of his clumsy attempts to write" (page 263) because he was writing about nothing which "had anything to do with what he had seen and felt and known" and so he turned to a subject within "his vision of the earth." His notion was to write a book encompassed by "a boy's vision of life over a ten-month period between his twelfth and thirteenth year, and the title was, 'The End of the Golden Weather.' "

On Fourteenth Street, Monk wrote and read, and observed life, and dreamed "golden fantasies" in which rich ladies, "twenty-four or five years of age (for he could not stand them younger than he was)," gave themselves to him. He abandoned friends like Jim Randolph and Jerry Alsop, the latter having preceded him to New York and established himself with a "new coterie" of virtuous fledglings.

&§ §&

Two distinct cycles, Wolfe wrote in *The Story of a Novel,* were defined in his giant manuscript "The October Fair." The first cycle, published as *Of Time and the River,* dealt with a "period of wandering and hunger in a man's youth. The second cycle described the period of greater certitude, and was dominated by the unity of a single passion." This, as we know, became the last four hundred pages of *The Web and the Rock.* It constituted a variation on the ancient theme of the youthful intellectual and the mature, understanding woman.

In August, 1925, after two years in New York and one abroad and with the inheritance from his father dissipated, George Webber came back home, only to discover he had no "home" to come back to. He had gone away to seek the "continental Golden Fleece," but he returned "a shorn Jason," his hands empty. Aged twenty-four and forced to go to work, he accepted a teaching position at the School of Utility Cultures.

On the voyage back he had a shipboard affair with Esther Jack, jolly, middle-aged, three-fourths Jewish, and a wife and mother. Monk fell in love with her, soon began to think of her as the most beautiful woman he had ever seen, and back in New York the two met frequently. She seemed to him a clever and "immensely talented creature of action, able to hold her own in a man's world"; for Esther was a well-known designer of clothes, theatrical costumes, and stage scenery. She represented a society which he craved but had never known, a society of wealth, prominence, and culture. She represented the Jewish world of good living, of art and travel, of richness and abundance.

More important than these considerations, however, Monk got from Esther a sureness of love which tempered his uneasiness and made him stable and contented. Her motherly strength and aesthetic sensitiveness were down to earth, giving him the direction and necessary discipline for his furious writing. By now his novel was enlarged from its original intent to cover the whole episode of Libya Hill. Constantly he worked on it in the skylighted room over a tailor's shop, where he lived and where Esther had a work desk with her design instruments nearby. There she came each day at noon to cook for him ("There is no spectacle on earth more appealing than that of a beautiful woman in the act of cooking dinner for someone she loves"), and there they made love and were happy. For the first time in his life, we are told, he was deeply and earnestly important to someone else.

> He had a sense of inner security, of self-belief, that he had not had before. And he believed in himself because someone else believed in him. His war with the world was somewhat abated because his own war with himself was reconciled. . . . The woman had, in fact, begun to give a kind of frame, design, and purpose to his life that it had never had before.

99

Aside from their personally satisfying hours together, Esther was still in Monk's mind the symbol of the city, the *rock*, "a kind of new America," the world of luxuries and theaters and restaurants and lovely women. She was the fashionable world of famous actresses and writers and painters and musicians and powerful financiers. She was all that, and she was a joyful worker, too, who delighted in everything she did. But wherever they went with each other, to the theater or to a smart gathering, Monk was aware of the chasm separating them. In spite of all his years in the city, he was still of the *town*, the sensitive, innocent, and puritanical provincial who would never be anything else. The only common element holding them together in this clash of two opposing environments was a certain naïveté of Esther's which always illumined her even when in the midst of her sophisticated and arrogant set. Monk thought that her talents were being patronized by the pompous devotees of the arts, and he resented it and wanted to tear her away. In such company, even when Esther was not involved, he writhed upon hearing one bejewelled quack comment condescendingly about a recent play, "It's rather good O'Neill. I think you might be interested."

As a result of his scorn for the artistic pretenders who were her friends, Monk began to quarrel with Esther. Harsh words arose, too, from a realization of his dependence on her. His love was a weblike "prison of the spirit." He sought to escape from it by unreasonable attacks on the only one who believed in his genius. When he saw in her the tangible emblem of the corruption into which he felt himself being drawn, he became crazed. The scoundrels she introduced him to were, he convinced himself, the most despicable of rotten impostors: charlatans like Van Vleeck (Carl Van Vechten) and Rosalind Bailey (Elinor Wylie) and Seamus Malone (Ernest Boyd). In these pages Wolfe's bitterly severe caricature of certain literary figures of the 1920's is annihilating.

Monk's defeat by the enemy was complete when the publishing firm of Rawng and Wright turned down his novel. He was not consoled even when Esther rescued the manuscript from destruction and turned it over to the agent Lulu Scudder (Madeleine Boyd). By the spring of 1928 his illusions were shattered; he thought himself "castrated" by Esther and her cynical crowd; he argued that she renewed her youth at his expense; yet he rationalized that it was the madness of "self-inflicted jealousy" which gave him these notions. He called her ugly names, chased her into the street, and shut her away from him though he still loved her. Unheeded went Esther's denials, her pleas that he should wisely use his life and talents and let them be "guided by a clear design."

After the recriminations and violence, the final break was quiet. One day Monk discovered that he had lost his "squeal," which from his childhood had symbolized the animal exuberance within him and which was always expressed by "a wild goat-cry of pain and joy and ecstasy." His squeal—a comical word, Monk realized—had left him when his novel was returned by the first publisher who read it. Time was when the cry "had united him to the whole family of the earth," and now in what he believed to be his personal failure, it had been lost because the human family had rejected him.

The moment for getting away had come, and George Webber sailed for Europe with the purpose of forgetting Esther and of recovering that which had been forfeited. He went to England, then Paris. "He had come away to forget her: he did nothing but remember her."

At Munich, during the Oktoberfest, when the new beer was "almost twice as strong as ordinary," he went to the great halls and drank deeply of the brew. The Germans, swinging their mugs and singing, were "a ring of savage, barbaric faces bent down above him." One evening, following a drunken fight, he awoke in a hospital.

In a sobering moment he looked at himself in the mirror of the little room. The image in the glass was Body, that is, Monk in time and space—a Body with limited possibilities, unable because of physical limitations to keep up with the other Monk, the spirit that is, which had no relationship to time and space but was always hungering for more than Body would allow. Both reflected on the origin within them of the Worm, defined by Louis D. Rubin as the "anxiety and discontent" resulting from the impossibility of maximum receptivity by the senses. The spirit yearned beyond the periphery of Body to receive. Both spirit and Body agreed that the best period for this receptivity was in youth when

> ". . . the sunlight came and went upon the porch, and when there was a sound of people coming home at noon. . . . That was a good time then."
> "Yes," said Body. "But—you can't go home again."

With these words, with this healthy mutual understanding between spirit and Body, the novel ends.

❧ ☙

Throughout *The Web and the Rock* there is a duality which operates on a number of levels. In the first place, there are the two unconnected parts which seem even more disjointed because of the lapse of time between their writing. The Monk of Libya Hill and the Monk of New York are almost two different persons. Second, two cultures are always opposed: among others, town and city, Gentile simplicity and Jewish opulence. Then, too, in Monk and Esther, Wolfe contrasts youth and age, innocence and sophistication.

This duality, even so, fails to build a new character out of Monk. Unlike Eugene Gant, he is shadowy and objectionably egocentric. It is difficult for a reader to sympathize with his self-torture, his invented prejudices, his madness, and most of all his shabby treatment of Esther. If his sensitivity and physical strangeness set him apart from other people, if acquaintances and those who loved him failed always to bow immediately before his unproved genius, Monk was no different from thousands of other American youths. Monk's agonies are more culpable, by far, than the bouncing hungers of Eugene Gant.

Unsatisfactory as all these things are, *The Web and the Rock* is, of course, a necessary link in the Wolfe saga. In that last chapter, one feels, Monk (or Wolfe-Gant) looks at himself honestly and sensibly for the first time. Within a half hour he is no longer a boy, but has become a man. Romanticism (subjectivity) has been altered, regrettably perhaps, into realism (objectivity). The transition was made quietly but it was finally made. And the one who is basically responsible for it is Esther Jack, one of Wolfe's great living creations. Her tragic misfortune was to love a man almost twenty years younger than she, and to love him beyond his belief in himself.

Aside from the incompletely realized hero of the book, other weaknesses are obvious. Excursive essays, like those in the first sections, continue intruding upon the narrative. Often there is no preparation for some significant phase of the story: as when suddenly Monk, without apprenticeship, is said to be putting his main strength into writing a novel; or when in the Old Pinakothek in Munich, never having been warned that he had any interest in art, we are abruptly given paragraphs on Monk's sensuous appreciation of painting. "He almost pulled Mathias Grünewald from the wall; he walked straight out of there carrying those lovely naked girls of Lucas Cranach in his brain." And not once in Munich—after Monk's convulsive pangs in England and France—is there a mention of Esther, though we were told so defiantly that in Europe "he did nothing but remember her." But, then, much of "Oktoberfest" belongs to *Of Time and the River*. This fault of Wolfe's in looking backward is awkwardly balanced by a looking forward: for instance, Monk's sympathy, following the break with Esther, for the downtrodden—a distinguishing characteristic of *You Can't Go Home Again* but not of its predecessors.

One of the aspects of *The Web and the Rock* in which the author is not remiss is the "strong element of satiric exaggeration" which, he announced in his prefatory note, he planned to have because it belonged "to the nature of life, and particularly American life." His satire of the New York literati has already been mentioned. With equal vigor he derided the Agrarians in Southern universities, issuing publications in which they extolled "the earthly virtues of both root and source in such unearthly language, by such processes of aesthetic subtlety, that even the cult adepts of the most precious city cliques were hard put to it to extract the meaning." Wolfe poked fun at professional Southerners like Jerry Alsop (the name itself is symbolic, as are many of the proper names in the novel) and at Southern actors and playwrights who slunk home at the first hint of failure in the North. Certainly *The Web and the Rock* contains some of Wolfe's most stinging satire of the false, the pompous, and the defeated.

Because his desire for objectivity was so determined, there are fewer strains of prose-poetry in the book. Yet Wolfe (through George Webber) was still exploring for "the substance of his own America . . . still seeking home." In the last pages the poetic fantasy of Body and spirit foreshadows an end of the search. The great discovery, finally, would be made in *You Can't Go Home Again.*

❧

Three books by Aline Bernstein provide a curious footnote to *The Web and the Rock*. In *Three Blue Suits* (1933) there is a six-page love story titled "Eugene." On reading it, Wolfe objected to the piece as "describing habits of disorder and confusion in my life and giving other information about me which was so unmistakable that no one who knew me could fail to identify me." In February, 1938, *The Journey Down* was published. This novel, an extended treatment of the love affair between a young writer and an older woman, parallels fairly closely the Monk-Esther chapters of *The Web and the Rock*. Evidently Mrs. Bernstein, knowing that Wolfe eventually would publish a fictional account of their years together, decided to "get the jump on him" by issuing her version first. *Miss Condon* (1947), a second novel, is the story of a woman's struggle between her love for her husband and for a young American whom she met abroad.

6

"YOU CAN'T GO HOME AGAIN"

A<small>LTHOUGH</small> the action of Wolfe's fourth novel follows hard upon the action of the third, there is a change of emphasis. As Wolfe carried his autobiographical story forward, a theme which persisted and recurred and hammered away in his brain without his knowing exactly what it meant was the notion that there is no going home again, no turning back, no reliving time. In *You Can't Go Home Again,* this theme seems, finally, to crystallize the notion.

When he visited Asheville in 1937, the former fascination with his birthplace vanished. "I was a citizen of Asheville," he wrote in spite of his self-exile, and then added, "and I am now a citizen of mankind." Of course, such a reflection was typical of the 1930's; for Wolfe, even so, it symbolized the whole of his last book. Five days before he set out from New York on that trip to the Far West which would never bring him back to the city, his abundant manuscript happily and securely deposited with the editor at Harpers, he wrote his literary agent Elizabeth Nowell: "I have not felt such hope and confidence in many years. It may be that I have come through a kind of transition period in my life—I believe this is the truth—and have now, after a lot of blood-sweat and anguish, found a kind of belief and hope and faith I never had before." It was a moment of certitude. If Wolfe had lived, he would have gone on searching for other values; but, at least for that day, the quest was at an end.

On its publication in 1940, *You Can't Go Home Again* was joyfully received in some quarters as long-awaited evidence that Thomas Wolfe had at last matured. It was this book, not *The Web and the Rock,* which discharged his promise of objectivity. While it is difficult to define literary maturity, and it is speculative, certainly, to attest whether maturity is always desirable, no one can deny Wolfe's shift in emphasis. Like a scholar, George Webber began to see relationships and associations and resemblances in all aspects of life. "Each new sensation and impression," we are told, "was no longer a single, unrelated thing: it took its place in a pattern and sifted down to form certain observable cycles of experiences." Instead of nursing a passionate solicitude for himself, Webber had thoughts and eyes always turning outwards. In a Christian sense, he found himself when he looked with pity and sympathy upon others.

This lessening of self-concentration was accompanied by a diminishing of lyric exuberance in style. Only occasionally in *You Can't Go Home Again* does youthful enthusiasm bubble through into poetry. In its place was a personal research into problems about him, into situations in which he was merely a single minor character or a lone observer: American business practices, economic fluctuations, race, international politics. One does not write poetry when reporting the findings of investigation.

Examination of one type of episode after another (the novel is divided into seven sections) shows that Wolfe had his hero Webber reach a conclusion following each of them. The novel, on this plan, is a series of rejections and a final acceptance. Discarded as insufficient are (in this order): blind hometown allegiance, privilege and love, praise and success, social uninvolvement, Fame, man's inhumanity to his fellows, and fatalistic determinism. At the end, by a process of elimination, Webber can cry out his Whitmanian belief in a "mystical evolution" toward betterment.

In the poetic statement which prefaces the first chapter, Wolfe recorded that it "seemed to him that all man's life was like a tiny spurt of flame that blazed out briefly in an illimitable and terrifying darkness, and that all man's grandeur, tragic dignity, his heroic glory, came from the brevity and smallness of this flame." *You Can't Go Home Again* is the affirmation of this tragic glory.

ঙ৯ ৫৯

In April, 1929, George Webber was back in New York, a half year after that conversation with himself in Munich. Henceforth he resolved to acknowledge his limitations, to consolidate his emotions and reason, and to prevent his life and love from coalescing. He would continue to see Esther, but he would not allow his passions to dominate him. Furthermore, he had reached a sort of jubilant independence, for Lulu Scudder had placed his novel *Home to Our Mountains* (*Look Homeward, Angel*) with the publishing firm of James Rodney & Company (Scribners). The resulting expansiveness of spirit led him to feel a common brotherhood with man—with the tiny Japanese artist Mr. Katamoto who lived below his quarters on Twelfth Street, with the nighttime truck drivers, and with the little men leaning on the sills of evening in the city.

On the train taking him to Aunt Maw's funeral, George met a group of Libya Hill boosters proclaiming the great future of his home town. The mayor, the leading banker, and a behind-the-scenes political manipulator greeted George and others on the train with chatter of real-estate values, insisting that they come back home again to settle and make a fortune in investments. Such advice had no effect on Nebraska Crane, now a big-league baseball player, who said he planned to live on his land, not sell it in speculation.

Underneath the frantic talk of the men, George perceived a nakedness and fear, particularly when the shameless blind usurer Judge Bland railed at the trio as "pious Puritans" who had "virtuously betrayed their town and given their whole-souled services to the ruin of their fellow men."

After the funeral George stayed on for a visit with Randy Shepperton. The town was insane. Lots on undeveloped mountainsides were sold at monstrous prices one day, re-sold the next at twice the amount—all, of course, on paper. The town sot was acclaimed a sort of oracle, and consulted on whether to buy or sell. The booster excitement was responsible for George's being written up in the local newspaper as shortly to come out with a "romance of the Old South," and George feared for the time of reckoning in this as in other realities the citizens of Libya Hill would have to face. The finale of this turbulent intoxication was George's overhearing Randy's sales supervisor dress him down for not meeting his quota. Sell, whether people want the product of not! Sell, or be discharged! Be a go-getter in boom town, or give up! George realized that the town of his childhood was lost, the people in it lost, and this was his farewell.

Another farewell came on October 17, 1929, just a week before the stock market crash. In a long section entitled "The World That Jack Built" (the name Jack, of course, signifies money), Wolfe wrote one of his most vivid episodes. On that day Esther and her husband were entertaining at a resplendent party in their Park Avenue apartment a few blocks north of Grand Central. Reluctantly, George Webber decided to attend. He knew he would be ill at ease among the great figures from the city's artistic and financial circles, but Esther's importunity was not this time to be dismissed.

The day began with the Jacks' awakening in their sumptuous sleeping quarters nine flights up. Frederick Jack arose, groomed himself with care, thought about the "young Gentile fool" who was always telephoning his wife. With Jewish wisdom he knew the middle way; he valued "the sacred and inviolable stability of the family" above impulsive quarrels and decisions. Down the hall Esther awoke—immediately alert, happy, thinking of George, looking forward to the evening.

Plans were checked with the servants. Then, after a busy day, the guests arrived. Esther had arranged for the high point of the evening to be the presentation of a puppet circus by Piggy Logan (Alexander Calder). At that season, this odd spectacle was the rage of fashionable parties. The *pièce de résistance* of Mr. Logan's performance was a sword-swallowing act during which he slowly pressed a hairpin into the mouth of a doll till its side "was torn open and some of the stuffing began to ooze out." George and the others watched the act with increasing horror. The operation betokened decadence. Something was degenerate about this whole gathering of parasites battening on the lives of those beneath them helpless and sweating. George looked about and saw the privileged guests, and though he knew they were to be pitied, he also knew that he must leave Esther immediately and finally. If he gave in now, he would deny himself the whole truth and then he would not be able to "sing America."

As the evening waned, a fire broke out in the apartment building. Down the darkened staircase the guests sought safety; but the damage actually was slight, and the only casualties were two lowly elevator operators who had been imprisoned between the floors when some irresponsible person pulled the wrong switch and prevented their escape from the dense smoke. The privileged escaped unharmed.

Soon George left. He remembered his decision. He still loved Esther, but love was not enough. Her world was the world of phoney values and fatal illusions. Those who lived in her world, of course, did not so see it; they thought themselves "knowing, practical, and hard-headed." They did not trouble themselves about dishonesty and self-interest; they accepted them as concomitants of normal life. Like the people in Libya Hill, they bought and sold, and would not adjust to harsh reality, even when the falseness of their living was revealed. But for the artist, privilege and truth were two separate entities, and George was aware there was no common meeting ground. He knew that "honesty, sincerity, no compromise with truth—these were the essentials of any art—and a writer, no matter what else he had, was just a hack without them." A phrase kept recurring to him: "He who lets himself be whored by fashion will be whored by time." The affair with Esther was finished. For once and all, George renounced privilege; and if love was coupled with it, love too had to go.

There was, though, something else George wanted: Success. When *Home to Our Mountains* was published during the first week of November, the reviewers were quite warm in their praise. But hardly had the words been printed before he was besieged by a vapid mass of social climbers, celebrity-conscious nymphomaniacs, and lion hunters. His mild, hollow notoriety was acutely balanced, however, by an angry, resentful reception of the book in Libya Hill, where, though he had so hopefully yearned for approbation, he was now reviled by readers who thought he had exposed the ugly facts about them. This was not so. He had written only the *truth,* but had done it so well that they had mistaken the truth for facts. The people in Libya Hill were bewildered and shaken; the *truth* in his book had made them mad.

The reaction might have been milder if the publication of the novel had not coincided with the beginning of the Great American Depression. In March, 1930, came the calamitous bank failure in Libya Hill and the suicide of the mayor. Boosterism exploded like a balloon. The Libya Hill people were ruined materially and spiritually; they discovered that when their false values were taken from them, they had "no inner equivalent from which they might now draw new strength." To Randy Shepperton, who had lost his job, George despondently framed an explanation:

". . . . America went off the track somewhere—back around the time of the Civil War, or pretty soon afterwards. Instead of going ahead and developing along the line in which the country started out, it got shunted off in another direction— and now we look around and see we've gone places we didn't mean to go. Suddenly we realize that America has turned into something ugly—and vicious—and corroded at the heart of its power with easy wealth and graft and special privilege. . . . And the worst of it is the intellectual dishonesty which all this corruption has bred. People are *afraid* to think straight— *afraid* to face themselves—*afraid* to look at things and see them as they are. We've become like a nation of advertising men, all hiding behind catch phrases like 'prosperity' and 'rugged individualism' and 'the American way.' And the real things like freedom, and equal opportunity, and the integrity and worth of the individual—things that have belonged to the American dream since the beginning—they have become just words, too. The substance has gone out of them—they're not real any more."

Perhaps, thought George, a real thing, unmodifiable by the shifting years, was Fame. He had had a measure of success, and the taste of it was bitter. He would now go questing for the Fair Medusa.

Giving up his job at the School of Utility Cultures, he rented a flat in Brooklyn among the simple, anonymous, abandoned beings who lived there, he no less than any of them, and all so vastly different from those favored few at the Jacks' party. He worked and was a part of their living and was not any longer a rare person set apart because he was an artist. Through his own suffering in these years of want and poverty, George "came to share those qualities in the lives of people all around," as Wolfe wrote of his own experiences in *The Story of a Novel*— those qualities which led him to participation "in the common life of man."

For three years he prowled the unfamiliar haunts of Brooklyn and Manhattan, saw the homeless men hovering for warmth in public latrines only a stone's throw from the fortifications of

Wall Street. The awful human devastation, he sought out with sympathy almost frenzied. On Sunday street corners he watched the loiterers tensed with an optimism that "something is sure to happen." George mused on the strange enigma of American life "mixed of harshness and of tenderness, of innocence and of crime, of loneliness and of good fellowship, of desolation and of exultant hope, of terror and of courage, of nameless fear and of soaring conviction, of brutal, empty, naked, bleak, corrosive ugliness, and of beauty so lovely and so overwhelming that the tongue is stopped by it, and the language for it has not yet been uttered." And he was exultant in his knowledge that man, in spite of all his weaknesses, had belief in life and would survive and be triumphant.

Alfred Kazin calls Wolfe "the most alert novelist of depression America," for "his imagination had presented his own situation and the American situation as coeval."

During these Brooklyn years George's only close friend was his editor Foxhall Edwards. As their association developed, George began to discern in Fox the second, spiritual Father he had never really found; and Fox, who moved in a home environment of women—his wife, five daughters, and a maid—began to discover in George the son he had ever longed for. He was a man of many eccentricities. He never took off his hat, barely removing it in the bath or when sleeping. His peculiar preference ran to guinea hen for breakfast. Yet Fox, with all his oddness and with all his fondness for George, was resigned to life's never improving. True, he would go to any lengths "to save the savable . . . to cure the curable, to keep the good," but that which he considered to be lost, he had no interest in trying to rescue. This tragic sense was like that of Ecclesiastes.

George did not have this tragic sense. The difference in point of view was illustrated in the suicide jump from the twelfth story of Brooklyn's Admiral Francis Drake Hotel (Hotel St. George) of a man named C. Green, one of life's little unidentified ciphers—in short, an American. To Fox, this C. Green was only a representative of Eliot's hollow men, an expendable atom from the drifts. But to George, he was no less noble than the heroic Sir Francis Drake himself. Death was C. Green's "final and defiant gesture of refusal to remain" a cipher. In death C. Green had found identity, had become a Man as George was a man.

No man was a cipher. Nor ever again, after his sojourn in Brooklyn among the small people of the earth, could George Webber be socially uninvolved in the life of any human being. Rejected was the nonlife of isolation.

ᵛᵝ ᵝᵛ

Shortly after this realization, George left for England. Always he seemed to be shifting from "anchored loneliness" to "foot-loose voyagings" and back again. With his London apartment, where he settled to do some writing, he inherited a charwoman whose unpretentiousness, sense of order, and energy he quickly learned to esteem. More so in England than in America, there was a sharp division between the Big People and the Little People. Daisy Purvis was, of course, one of the Little People. She literally gave her life over to the interests of her employer and was as excited as he with the announcement of the approaching arrival of the great Lloyd McHarg.

McHarg, in that year probably the leading literary figure in America, had praised Webber in a speech (actually Sinclair Lewis' Nobel Prize acceptance) "as a future spokesman of his country's spirit"; and when the younger writer, vastly grateful, wrote his thanks, McHarg replied with a promise to see him on an impending visit to Europe. And so the day arrived when George got a telephone call that the great man was in town, eager to receive him at his hotel.

McHarg was not a handsome man. As George looked at him, he was "red"—hair, ears, eyebrows, eyelids, hands—everything. Though noticeably worn from a three-day carouse, he excitedly suggested to George that they go off at once on a visit to the English countryside.

George was alarmed that this paragon of Fame was unsettled,

disillusioned, disappointed, was continually on the move, drink-ing hard, pushing himself to exhaustion, that acclaim and pres-tige had not brought contentment, but George was cheered to note that he could still have goodness and nobility in him de-spite that which was "jangled, snarled, and twisted . . . bitter, harsh, and acrid" in his life. When the two got in a rented Rolls-Royce, McHarg collapsed completely. After a nightmare journey, they arrived at a country house where McHarg had to be carried to his room. George was charmingly entertained by McHarg's host—a pleasant man but one who had retreated from the struggles of a world he had not strength to face, not unlike his American equivalents who escaped into the country houses of Connecticut and Vermont. Half-men of the arts they were.

The next morning, McHarg, refreshed by sleep and rest, his vitality recouped, was ready to go back to the city. In London the two novelists said good-by. (On the publication of *You Can't Go Home Again,* Sinclair Lewis stated that Wolfe per-mitted himself a bounteous measure of literary license in the portrait of Lloyd McHarg.)

For George, this meeting with McHarg was sobering. Here was the "living embodiment of his own dearest and most secret dream"; and now, at "his first encounter in the flesh with that fair Medusa, Fame herself," the young man realized how worth-less the attainment could be. He would need to learn the lesson finally by an accomplishment of it for himself, but he was not unprepared for the emptiness it would bring.

Returning home from Europe, George readied his manuscript, gave it to Fox, then, shortly before publication, headed for Germany, the country "after America, which he liked the best." In Berlin his books had been highly honored, and he was a famous man. Called "the great American epic writer," he had conquered the Fair Medusa at last.

But there was something wrong in Germany—this romantic land where the quest of Fame had ended. At the Olympic games he saw the Leader, "a little dark man with a comic-opera mustache." While no one spoke out openly against the Nazis and George beheld no brutalities, there was a subtle "something full of horror" within this great race of "people who had been psychically wounded and were now desperately ill with some dread malady of the soul." The poison had crept into his friends and made them helpless. And so it was that Fame had come to him amid confusion; it, too, had to be rejected and he must leave.

When his train reached the Belgian border, an ill-tempered little Jew who had shared George's compartment was apprehended by the Nazi police for attempting to smuggle money from the country. The arrest epitomized the loss, to George, of his "dark, found Helen" (Germany), now shot through with barbaric "greed and lust and force." As the Jew was led away, a sense of enormous guilt arose in George. Along with his shame was a feeling of "farewell, not to a man, but to humanity; not to some pathetic figure, some chance acquaintance of the voyage, but to mankind; not to some nameless cipher out of life, but to the fading image of a brother's face." Not ever now would he be able to go home again, but always he would have to move outward to encircle humanity with an all-embracing compassion.

This terror which he had witnessed cried out fervently for self-appraisal, after which his place in the world—Thomas Wolfe's place in the world, for which he had been searching since the early pages of *Look Homeward, Angel*—would then and unmistakably and inevitably be clear. And suddenly it *was* clear. At last he knew what he was for.

One more step he had to take before freedom from the past was his: a breaking off with Foxhall Edwards. Of all the things he had ever faced, this would be the most painful. But it had to be done, and so he sat down and wrote Fox a long letter, hoping through self-examination to clarify his position for the editor and for himself as well.

First he reviewed his college years and the postwar decade. He denied belonging to the Lost Generation, for he no longer

felt lost. He observed that no one can "really be superior without humility and tolerance and understanding," and he re-
gretted the period in young manhood when he had assumed an
obviously false superiority. Then, later, when he had eagerly
wooed Love and Fame, he had come to know their emptiness.
His visit to Germany had taught him another lesson. In that
country there were the corrupters and the persecuted—far
worse than merely the rich and the poor of America. If in Germany truth was impossible, at least in America there was still
hope. All of these were avowals which hard experience had
brought him to.

There would never again be a looking homeward; in life, one
must go constantly forward. Here, fundamentally, was the reason why George and Fox must part. Though Fox's fatalism was
a hopeful one, he was nevertheless like Ecclesiastes the
Preacher; he was a man of resignation, of acceptance of things
as they are. Though he was infinitely gentle and kind and wise,
he was nevertheless firm in his belief that mankind was doomed
to evil and suffering and there was no help for it. George could
not accept that view. Even when he agreed with Fox that "Man
was born to live, to suffer, and to die" and that his lot on earth
was tragic to the end, there was a necessity to *"deny it all along
the way."* Time was Flux, not Fix. Everything changed, and
the changing man was Man-Alive, who must struggle with the
evils of the hour, never for a moment give in to them, but live
confidently in the precept that all things must change for the
better. "You and the Preacher may be right for all eternity, but
we Men-Alive, dear Fox, are right for Now. And it is for Now,
and for us the living, that we must speak, and speak the truth,
as much of it as we can see and know." Thus George must always be against the enemies of Men-Alive. In his transcendent
credo, his final affirmation:

> I believe that we are lost here in America, but I believe we
> shall be found. . . . I know that America and the people in it
> are deathless, undiscovered, and immortal, and must live.

I think the true discovery of America is before us. I think the true fulfillment of our spirit, of our people, of our mighty and immortal land, is yet to come. I think the true discovery of our own democracy is still before us. And I think that all these things are certain as the morning, as inevitable as noon. I think I speak for most men living when I say that our America is Here, is Now, and beckons on before us, and that this glorious assurance is not only our living hope, but our dream to be accomplished.

George knew that he must die, but his death would be only a drifting leaf in the vast changing process of humanity: "a wind is rising, and the rivers flow." Man-Alive would not die.

⋲§ §⋗

On February 14, 1938, three months before he laid his pen aside, Wolfe wrote to Edward Aswell concerning the manuscript he would shortly turn over to Harpers for inspection. Though the extensive pages of George Webber's adventures were later published in two volumes, on that day Wolfe spoke of his work as one book, "about one man's discovery of life."

And, in order that there may be no doubt as to what this process of discovery involves, the whole book might almost be called "You Can't Go Home Again"—which means back home to one's family, back home to one's childhood, back home to the father one has lost, back home to romantic love, to a young man's dreams of glory and of fame, back home to exile, to escape to "Europe" and some foreign land, back home to lyricism, singing just for singing's sake, back home to aestheticism, to one's youthful ideas of the "artist," and the all-sufficiency of "art and beauty and love," back home to the ivory tower, back home to places in the country, the cottage in Bermuda away from all the strife and conflict of the world, back home to the father one is looking for—to someone who can help one, save one, ease the burden for one, back home to the old forms and systems of things that once seemed everlasting, but that are changing all the time—back home to the escapes of Time and Memory. Each of these discoveries, sad

117

and hard as they are to make and accept, are described in the book almost in the order in which they are named here. But the conclusion is not sad: this is a hopeful book—the conclusion is that although you can't go home again, the home of every one of us is in the future: there is no other way.

I hope you will keep this description of the purpose of the book in mind and read it pretty carefully, and think about it a lot, because I am depending on you now so much. I want you to be thoroughly convinced at the outset that I know what I am doing and where I am going; and although there are many, many doubts in my mind, there is no doubt; and although there are many, many confusions, there is no confusion.

There was no confusion of fact in Wolfe's having come from a boy's doubts, a boy's need of home and security and assurance, to a man's realization that only through progression lay inevitable betterment. Felicity was possible, but only if one believed in its possibility and worked for it. This simple idea had dawned upon him with such staggering clarity that, in his excitement, he detailed no outline for exactly how this better world was to be achieved. Some readers have pointed out that the absence of a plan weakens his conclusion. On the other hand, one may contend that, now that full social consciousness was his, he might next have scheduled procedures. But this he lacked time to do. Meanwhile, with the old ways denied and blocked, he viewed the new, the only, the one way. And the essence of the way which he and all mankind had before them was the belief that it was there.

7

✌ OTHER WRITINGS

SINCE Wolfe generally spoke of his occupation as that of a "writer" or "artist," he was obviously, by virtue of that definition, far more concerned with the thing he had to tell and the way he had to tell it than he was with the kind of literary designation it eventually would assume. Always he was writing "the book"—a continuous literary production later to be shaped with the help of those who could best advise him.

Thus he rarely sat down to write a story with a formalized beginning, middle, and end. He wrote, at any one time, what he was then compelled to write. Such a routine, depending on impulse, was wasteful, as he well knew; but it was his way, and for him the only way, even when he realized that he was writing much, much more than ever would go into a published volume. The great collection of Wolfe manuscript in the Houghton Library at Harvard University contains numberless pages which never were and likely never will be printed. Many of them are rough, incomplete episodes not used anywhere. Others are early versions of material later reworked for publication. They are valuable primarily to the Wolfe scholar, not to the literary explorer who would bring to light some hidden Wolfe treasures.

Another characteristic of everything that went into "the book" was that it came out of Wolfe's own experience. Through an examination of his experience in life, he hoped to clarify his "vision" and to find his America, and he could not do these things if he tried to see with someone else's eyes. Consequently his four novels and his other writings, too, were all cut from the same cloth. Whatever he wrote—*almost* everything he put down on paper—was something which had happened to Thomas Wolfe. What, then, may often seem to be an isolated story is only a fragment of the Wolfe "book." It may be part of the Gant cycle, or the Webber cycle, but it fits somewhere.

This, but in a lesser sense, is true even of his undergraduate writings: the poems, the one-act plays of the mountaineers, and other juvenilia. Though Wolfe later expressed some shame for these unripe college productions—admittedly dashed off carelessly by a student who had more ability than wisdom—they are intriguing and curious documents, not primarily because they have an excellence of their own, but because of him who wrote them. Even the minor efforts of a significant writer possess interest, aside from any intrinsic qualities.

❦

His first major effort was *Welcome to Our City,* a play written in 1922–1923. In ten scenes loosely strung together, young Wolfe sketched a bitter caricature of Altamont, a Southern town ignominiously grasping for the Bigger and Better at any cost. The slight dramatic action opposed the aristocratic reactionary Rutledge, determined to regain his father's ancestral mansion on the hill above "Niggertown," and Dr. Johnson, the well-to-do Negro physician who currently owned it. In league with Rutledge were all the town boosters who schemed to dispossess the Negroes of a section of town which had become a desirable site for development. Johnson, after surprising Rutledge's son trying to seduce his mulatto daughter, retracted his agreement to sell. The Negroes fired the settlement, the National Guardsmen were called in, and Johnson was killed. The opportunists from the Board of Trade emerged as lone winners.

The play is not strictly, however, a drama of racial tensions. No altruistic hero defends the downtrodden; and the Negroes in the cast are analyzed for their weaknesses: the sanctimonious Uncle Toms, the reckless and ignorant irresponsibles, the organizers for Social Equality, and even the Dr. Johnsons of the race. Wolfe holds out little hope for them, even if they had not been confronted by inane Civil War veterans, phoney culture-promoters, and Chamber of Commerce secretaries quoting travel-pamphlet prose.

The play, in the spirit of the "Boom Town" section of *You Can't Go Home Again,* lampoons just about everybody, including the hollow, worthless Democratic nominee for governor, and even the professor dismissed for teaching evolution. The real-estate interests receive the major part of the blast.

Only a talented, fired-up, indignant collegian could have written *Welcome to Our City.* Its obvious defects in dramatic structure are well balanced by Wolfe's fiery satire. Though there is no record that it has ever been staged since the 47 Workshop showing, it was seriously considered for production in New York shortly after the time of its writing.

❧ ☙

Mannerhouse, a second full-length play, dates from the summer of 1923. Off and on Wolfe revised it and rewrote it till he suddenly started a novel three years later. In *Of Time and the River,* the autobiographical Eugene Gant reads this script to his friends at Far Field Farm. At that distance from its composition Wolfe termed it a "groping and uncertain play" which possessed yet "some of the real grandeur, beauty, terror, and unuttered loneliness of America."

The action begins in ante-bellum times, then follows through to postwar days, its subject, according to *Of Time and the River,* "the decline and fall and ultimate extinction of a proud old family of the Southern aristocracy." The hero, appropriately named Eugene, rebelliously stands by while his father, General Ramsay, builds a grand house and haughtily rules over his Negroes, his possessions, and his family. When war is declared, Eugene goes off to battle with his father, though he still feels that the old order is wrong. At war's end, with the Ramsay "kingdom" collapsed, the house is purchased by a former share-cropper, who then makes a slave of the returned Eugene. The new order, too, is unjust and, in a moment of resolution, Eugene, with Samsonlike strength, pulls a "column from its rotted base" and the great mansion falls upon those who are symbolically captured by it. Now a fresh, productive order is possible.

Wolfe admitted that the drama owed much to *The Cherry Orchard* and *Cyrano de Bergerac,* that the love scenes were reminiscent of Ophelia and Hamlet, and that the young hero was "a rather Byronic character"; but the playwright was too much a child of the 1920's to understand his indebtedness to O'Neill. In its pompous but grand dialogue, its gloomy theme and characters, its atmosphere of decay and doom, its struggle of youth with age, *Mannerhouse* could easily be one of O'Neill's minor efforts. More important, though, is a look at the embryonic Eugene Gant as set forth in the hero, hopelessly caught, in spite of his desire to escape, within the confines of environment and heredity.

Mannerhouse, rejected by the Theatre Guild and the Neighborhood Playhouse, had its première at Yale University on May 5, 1949. Since then, it has had successful professional productions in Germany.

&3 &o

The Story of a Novel is an expanded essay revealing the author's state of mind during the writing of *Look Homeward, Angel* and *Of Time and the River.* In addition to its vast importance to any student of Wolfe's art, it has been termed one of the most frankly confessional tracts in all literature. A good bit of the Wolfe legend finds its genesis here. Some of the extraordinary revelations outraged reviewers, and in some quarters are still shocking. Such a passage was the one in which Wolfe compared his creativity to "a huge black cloud" inside him, "swelling and gathering all the time." The "cloud was loaded with electricity, pregnant, crested, with a kind of hurricane violence that could not be held in check." Finally the cloud "opened up and, mid flashes of lightning," poured "from its depth a torrential and ungovernable flood." Many readers thought, What a way for a book to be written! In spite of objections, the metaphor is probably justified.

When matched with the *Letters,* the factual information in *The Story of a Novel* is at times simplified and at others somewhat exaggerated, and therefore not entirely trustworthy. For instance, in the essay Wolfe said he began *Look Homeward, Angel* in London. A note in *Hungry Gulliver* has Ilkley as the place. Daniel L. Delakas cites Paris, while if one is prone to follow *Of Time and the River* as autobiography, it was at Tours.

But more significant than material for a minor debate like this is the narrative of Wolfe's emotional plight from the moment he first undertook prose fiction. There is no need to question the tortures and delights he experienced in getting *Look Homeward, Angel* on paper, nor to doubt his agony concerning the reception of the book in Asheville. Fully described are his dreams of Time and Guilt as he got its sequel under way, the year he spent with Perkins shaping *Of Time and the River,* the enormous cuts demanded of the manuscript, the writing of unfinished parts, and then his fear of publication and the persistent notion that delay would allow him to perfect the book.

The Story of a Novel was based on lectures Wolfe gave at the University of Colorado in August, 1935, and in expanded form was printed serially in the *Saturday Review of Literature* before book publication.

❧ ❧

From Death to Morning, a collection of previously printed short pieces, was issued by Scribners late in 1935 in order to capitalize on the popular reception of *Of Time and the River.*

Throughout, the major theme is loneliness, not surprising since Wolfe wrote most of these stories during his Brooklyn withdrawal. In the midst of the noisy, lusty, brawling millions of South Brooklyn, he experienced a physical alienation which accentuated his earlier concept of man's aloneness. In "No Door" and "Only the Dead Know Brooklyn" the vast area is undiscovered even by the "pavement ciphers" who people it. In the episodic "Death of the Proud Brother" Wolfe assumes a sort of Whitmanian identification with four human beings whose deaths he witnessed, all of them little, seemingly unimportant creatures of the day: a drunken bum, a pushcart vendor run down by a truck, a rivet-catcher falling from a building, and an anonymous fellow man found dead in a subway.

Several of the selections in *From Death to Morning* were apparently culled from the rejected pages of *Look Homeward, Angel.* "The Men of Old Catawba" is a fictitious history of the hero's native state, a tale of men "living and dying alone in the wilderness." In "The Four Lost Men" a first-person Eugene Gant listens to his father's comments on great names from the recent past; and the refrain "Garfield, Arthur, Harrison, and Hayes" sets Eugene to reflections on the youth of these giants. Did they, like all young Americans, have yearnings and fierce hopes? "The Face of War" is a series of tragic episodes in the violent, empty lives of those whom Eugene encountered during the summer of 1918 at Langley Field.

A meditative nostalgia infuses such short-short-stories as "The Bums at Sunset," in which Wolfe communicates the friendliness existing among those who wander the "lonely distances of America," and as "The Far and the Near," about the railroad engineer's affection for a nameless family who waved to him each day on his run. The commonplace good-bys exchanged at the Munich railway station, in "Dark in the Forest, Strange as Time," brings the writer a haunting kinship with his father's dark Germany. There are other similar sketches.

The strictly autobiographical "Gulliver" reveals how lonely and separate a six-foot-six titan feels in a five-foot-eight world.

Yet somehow, Wolfe explains, this very isolation eventually gave him an "inexplicable" faith in mankind.

About his 100-page novelette "The Web of Earth," a masterly texture of family history and mountain violence, Wolfe once wrote that it concerned "an old woman, who sits down to tell a little story, but then her octopal memory weaves back and forth across the whole fabric of her life until everything has gone into it." The narrator, of course, is Eliza Gant—garrulous, folksy, superstitious, earthy—talking to her son Eugene in Brooklyn. This skillfully conceived monologue hinges on two voices Eliza heard the year the locusts came. "Two . . . Two," said one, and the other, "Twenty . . . Twenty." In between the introduction of these strains and the revelation of their mysterious meanings, Eliza harks back to her husband's two early marriages, to his love of abundance and his drunken sprees. When her union with him changed to a lost, worthless thing, she held on valiantly to her children and to the land. Readers of *Look Homeward, Angel* who have perhaps misunderstood Eliza and failed to recognize her stamina and courage have in this story the portrait of the amazing, gallant woman Wolfe intended her. "Two . . . Two" and "Twenty . . . Twenty." At first Eliza thought the voices had to do with the warning she received twenty minutes before a pair of mountain murderers came to her house. Later she grasped a deeper interpretation; for, twenty days from the night of the murderers, "at twenty minutes to ten o'clock on the seventeenth day of October, *twins* were born—Ben and Grover were both born that night."

It may be that "The Web of Earth" with its unity and suspense and well-wrought narrative line, is Wolfe's most artistic single achievement.

᪗ ᪘

The Hills Beyond, a second collection of miscellaneous pieces, some having appeared in periodicals, some not, was brought out in 1941, the last publication of Wolfe's fiction. The contents of this third posthumous volume, according to editor Edward Aswell, who provided a valuable "Note" as appendix, represented the best of Wolfe which had not previously been issued in book form. In addition to ten short selections, there is the 150-page title story, "The Hills Beyond," comprising the first chapters of a novel on which the author was working at the time of his death.

Three of the six stories which belong to the Gant cycle are among Wolfe's most sensitive compositions. "The Lost Boy" is a four-angled view of Ben's twin brother Grover, the eleven-year-old who died at St. Louis during the Fair. First is a touching episode of the boy and his father in Altamont; then the reader sees him from Eliza's eyes (". . . the best boy I had—the smartest boy I ever saw—was—well, it wasn't Eugene . . . —the best of the lot was—Grover!"); then the older sister tells of the boy's illness and death; and finally Eugene, in St. Louis years and years later, returns to the house where Eliza and her brood lived for seven months in 1904 ("The years dropped off like fallen leaves: the face came back again—the soft dark oval, the dark eyes, the soft brown berry on the neck, the raven hair, all bending down, approaching—the whole appearing to him ghost-wise, intent and instant"), and there at the house, Eugene, now grown, recaptures Time, knowing even then that the "lost magic would not come again."

Also in the Gant cycle, as expert as this story but in technique quite different, is "Chickamauga," in which Wolfe relates the experiences of two mountain youths in the Civil War, centering on that great battle in the cedar thicket. John Pentland, the narrator, is the author's own great-uncle in Yancey County, North Carolina, with whose words, Wolfe said, he told the story in almost verbatim dialect. In the first part of "The Return of the Prodigal" Eugene describes an imaginary homecoming and the disgrace caused by his book, and his renting a room for a night in his mother's boarding house, where even she did not recognize him. In the second part is the actual return. After edging upon Altamont from the county seat (Burnsville) of Zebulon (Yancey) County, where he witnessed a mountain fight, Eugene musters the courage to go into his home town. There, to his amazement, he is overwhelmed with attention. "The only ones who are mad today," he is told in reference to his book, "are those you left out."

"No Cure for It" has Eugene, at seven, growing tall like a weed and resembling a monkey—foreshadowing the image of George Webber. In "Gentlemen of the Press," written as a one-act play, we have another Wolfean picture of Nighttime Americans, now in the newspaper office of a small city. Ben Gant is present. A reporter spins the mountain legend that Abraham Lincoln, spirited incognito to Yancey County after Waterloo, is really the son of Napoleon and Maria Louisa. "A Kinsman of the Blood" belongs to the Bascom Pentland section of *Of Time and the River*.

The other short selections in *The Hills Beyond* attach loosely to the Webber cycle. "On Leprechauns" contrasts America's neglect of talented and hard-working native authors with the nineteen-twenties' fad for mediocre Irish literary figures. "Portrait of a Literary Critic" satirizes a typical "practitioner of middle-of-the-roadism" with his silly dicta that Joyce and Faulkner are obscene novelists, "Sex is Dull," the "true art-expression of America was the comic strip," and the "only music that was real was Jazz." A great banker, sold out to success and a wife, is pictured in "The Lion at Morning."

That Wolfe was a man without religion—an opinion sometimes heard—is denied by the autobiographical essay "God's Lonely Man," in which he tells of searching the Bible for consolation and discovery. Though Christ's teachings, he concluded, were to destroy loneliness and establish love, his own belief was that loneliness was "the central and inevitable fact of human existence." Aswell, who knew the writer better than anyone that last year, wrote that Wolfe "was a deeply religious man in the unconventional and truest sense of the word."

To the uncompleted novel "The Hills Beyond," much attention has been directed by those who saw evinced in its ten

Wolfe in Colorado, August 10, 1935   *Pack Library*

chapters Wolfe's final and complete turning away from his autobiographical heroes. In truth, only wraiths of Eugene-George tremble among its pages, and its animus is more that of "The Web of Earth" and "Chickamauga" than *Look Homeward, Angel* and *The Web and the Rock*.

The Publisher's Note in *Of Time and the River* mentions two projected Wolfe novels which would dip back into history with limited time-spans: The Hills Beyond Pentland (1838–1926) and Pacific End (1791–1884). Later, when he threw over Eugene Gant, and when he discovered how much of his "family history" had been used here and there, he abandoned the series. Yet he did not relinquish the desire to write a novel emphasizing the entanglements within a Southern family rather than the adventures of one hero, and he furthermore was eventually faced with providing George Webber with some ancestors. "The Hills Beyond" was his thrust in that direction.

Dropping the name Pentland as a reminder of the Gant series, he moved into the mountains of Zebulon County for origins and came up with old William "Bear" Joyner—shoeless pioneer "increate with myth," husband of two wives, father of more than twenty children, bear-fighter, and a man of incredible feats. When a courthouse was located at Libya Hill, old "Bear" put down stakes, bringing along four sons of his Presbyterian first wife and leaving the offspring of his Baptist second wife behind in the hills. At his store, which prospered, he established son Rufus as the tradesman. Zachariah (modeled on Governor Zebulon Vance of North Carolina) and Robert (on Vance's brother Robert) went to college, became lawyers, and assumed prominence, Zack a fun-loving, down-to-earth governor and United States senator, Robert a Superior Court judge. A fourth son, Theodore (Colonel Robert Bingham), went to war, founded a military school, and married a Virginia lady.

After delineating these rich hill-born characters drawn from famous mountain personalities, Wolfe obviously intended going back to Zebulon County and tracing the Baptist Joyners; for Monk Webber's grandfather Lafayette, barely mentioned, is to sire Amelia, who will, as we know from *The Web and the Rock,* marry John Webber from Pennsylvania. John Webber is introduced in the seventh chapter, a "brick mason and general builder" with a "big torso" and strong hands, "simian in his short legs"—a man soon in the good graces of the influential town Joyners. The story of how the town and country Joyners got along with each other, of how Webber met Amelia, was never written.

The completed chapters pose no romantic Southern chronicle. Wolfe makes clear that his mountain people "were a backwoods folk—a small-farm, hunting, hewing, clearing, trapping, and log-cabin sort of people." Wolfe has come a long way from the rose-tinted, tragic aristocrats of *Mannerhouse.* Few of the Old Catawbans in "The Hills Beyond" had ever owned slaves, though in Reconstruction times the contemptible Confederate professionals pretended that they had. Wolfe's spokesman is Judge Robert Joyner, who hated the laziness, ignorance, and pretense of the nonprogressive veterans.

Still, it was all part of the map of a section of America; and in one of his now-seldom paeans, Wolfe utilized the mountain courthouse as a symbol:

> The county courthouse was, in short, America—the wilderness America, the sprawling, huge, chaotic, criminal America. It was murderous America soaked with murdered blood, tortured and purposeless America, savage, blind, and mad America, exploding through its puny laws, its pitiful pretense. It was America with all its almost hopeless hopes, its almost faithless faiths—America with the huge blight on her of her own error, the broken promise of her lost dream and her unachieved desire; and it was America as well with her unspoken prophecies, her unfound language, her unuttered song. And just for all these reasons it was for us all our own America—with all her horror, beauty, tenderness, and terror—with all we know of her that never has been proved, that has never yet been uttered—the only one we know, the only one there is.

This familiar poetic richness, however, is infrequent in "The Hills Beyond." In spite of the salty Joyner clan, and the mountain yarns and graphic episodes, this fragment of Wolfe's last novel too often seems contrived, its prose purposely low-pressured, and its narrative mannered and selective. Good as it might have been from another writer—if this is the studied objectivity toward which Wolfe's critics pushed him, they did him a disservice.

❧ ☙

A Western Journal (1951) is Wolfe's account of a thirteen-day automobile trip in late June, 1938, through eight states in the company of two companions, hitting briefly the National Parks. Never intended for publication, the almost illegible draft was hurriedly scrawled out each night in hotels and tourist lodges. Later Wolfe obviously intended filling out his notes with characterizations. In its unrevised state, the diary provides us with the raw flow of Wolfe's prose—the color, the flamboyant vocabulary, and the spontaneous iambics.

Leaving Portland on June 20, the three travelers raced down Oregon, Yosemite their destination; then they sped across the Mojave Desert to Grand Canyon—"Big Gorgooby," Wolfe nicknamed it, and at night it was "immensely, darkly, almost weirdly there—a fathomless darkness peered at from the very edge of hell with abysmal starlight." In Utah he met with a "quaint old blondined wag named Florence who imitates bird calls and dark rather attractive woman, Canadian probably French, who sold curios and who had life in her—and was obviously willing to share it—" On July 2, after a snowy overnight on Mt. Rainier, the trip ended in Seattle. Wolfe had seen thousands of new American miles, and he ended his journal ". . . the pity, terror, strangeness, and magnificence of it all."

Four days later he became ill. Except for a letter to Maxwell Perkins, these were his last written words.

❧ ☙

Two volumes of letters have been published: *Thomas Wolfe's Letters to His Mother* (1943) and *The Letters of Thomas Wolfe* (1956). Both collections project a man who, completely at ease with the written word, chose, whenever he could, to explore situations and provide solutions on paper rather than keep them in his mind or talk them out.

The first of these books, if read immediately after *Look Homeward, Angel,* furnishes a sound appreciation of the difference between fact and autobiographical fiction. The letters are not unlike those of any young man writing to a mother on whom he is partially dependent. There are endless pages on expenses and economies, as there are routine comments on the weather, and tidbits of family news. Here, also, is the story of Asheville's resentment after *Look Homeward, Angel* was published, and the sure proof that Wolfe conceived of his Gant characters as *great* people. If he was sometimes critical of his family, he was nevertheless inextricably bound to them by admiration and the strongest blood ties.

The second book, a generous and judicious selection to all correspondents except his mother and Aline Bernstein, reads, as has been said, like Wolfe's "last novel." Included are many letters written in indignation, but unmailed in the bright sunlight of the next day. Literary invective has a two-fisted holiday. Among writers for whom he had no use are H. L. Mencken, Bernard De Voto, T. S. Eliot, Thornton Wilder, Ezra Pound, and Ernest Hemingway. *Gone With the Wind* is "that immortal piece of bilge." While names of prominent people are printed uninhibitedly, editor Elizabeth Nowell was overly and unfortunately cautious with lesser figures. This aspect of her editing results in many annoying and unnecessary ellipses.

The dominant impression of both volumes is that of a man totally dedicated to the life of the artist. Through love and ecstasies, disappointment and depression, Wolfe's life was an undiminishing struggle to overcome those obstacles which blocked the direction he, tortured by his unequal race with Time, felt his energies must take.

8

⸙ IN CONCLUSION

I<small>N THE</small> twelve years between the time he began to write
Look Homeward, Angel in 1926 and his death in 1938, Wolfe
turned out literally millions of words. It is a record few major
American writers, past or present, can equal. The reason for
this enormous output is found in Wolfe's obsession to write,
write, write. When he was writing, he endured a rather contented hell; yet, even when exhausted, he thought only of the
time when he would be writing again. The necessary but arid
intervals separating the periods of writing were less than contented hells, for he was not happy to be idle and his repeated
denunciations of himself for laziness were mere self-recrimina-
tions for not having done more.

What sort of novelist this prolific author might have been
in another era of American writing is useless speculation. He
was a man of his day, and he fitted himself to his hour and his
personality. Sometimes it seems odd that, despite attempts of
some literary historians to force him into a category with the
naturalists or the neo-romantics or what you will, Wolfe never
manages to rest in any of the slots very comfortably. Even-

tually he pries his way out. He never belonged to any writers' school or clique—a defiance he repeatedly shouted to protect his individuality—and as early as 1931 was proclaiming that "the only standard I will compete against now is in me."

Yet Wolfe was neither out of space nor out of time. His first two novels are clear products of the 1920's, the last two of the 1930's. As a matter of fact, Eugene Gant was a johnny-come-lately at the tag end of a host of romantic escapists in the literature of the twenties. The rebellious spirit of Sherwood Anderson's influential *Winesburg, Ohio* (1919) and Sinclair Lewis's widely read *Main Street* (1920) infused a whole generation of writers with a dissatisfaction with the small town. Fictional heroes, weary with constrictions, lashed out at conventional middle-class morality and angrily denounced the falseness of Puritanical America. Liberation, creation, experience—these were the desiderata; and the young heroes ground between their teeth the boorishness of the village and set off for the cities or for abroad or, as did Eugene at first, for Harvard. Not for nothing had Dreiser's Sister Carrie, twenty years earlier, ridden a train into freedom by way of Chicago and Montreal and New York. There was little difference between the protagonists of fiction and the authors themselves. In *The Story of a Novel* a seasoned Wolfe said that, after all, the flights to Europe were not so much an escape from "the Philistinism, the materialism, and ugliness of American life which we said we were fleeing from, but from the necessity of grappling squarely with ourselves and the necessity of finding in ourselves, somehow, the stuff to live by, to get from our own lives and our own experience the substance of our art."

At any rate, the idealistic heroes, in their rush for a compulsive, vigorous release, could no longer bear physical or spiritual confinement. Abandoning their home towns, though they could never sell or even give away their birthrights, they cast aside (or thought they did, or at least they tried to) the whole gamut of provincial and accepted dogma. In this deliberate breaking with the past—an action essentially the attitude of the romantics—the creators of these *new* heroes assiduously cut the attaching cords. Even the old art was not good enough. As constructive iconoclasts, they sought their peculiar directions; and in the 1920's American literature launched such diverse novelists as Fitzgerald, Hemingway, Faulkner, Caldwell, and Wolfe, all of whom in their different ways discovered their own styles and their own forms. No one of them can be judged by the standards which another set for himself.

Then came the 1930's. It has been said that much of serious American writing begins in dissatisfaction, then casts about for a more tolerable way of life. So it was that the 1930's gave novelists a choice opportunity to continue their revolt, the emphasis shifting to social and economic problems. Wolfe, sidetracking for the moment his search for lasting values, focused his attack on the structure of his society, which he felt had waged a successful and relentless war on its members. His attack became a very real conflict with the Enemy World; and the projection of his private battle into a universal concept was, certainly for him, possible only in terms of the society which he observed and in which he lived. Prisoner as he was to the proletarian resentment of the Great Depression years, particularly in *You Can't Go Home Again* he was not out of step with revolutionaries like Henry Miller, Farrell, Steinbeck, and O'Hara.

Still, Wolfe was unlike all of them except Miller in that he was not, as Kazin notes, a novelist *of* society. Like Miller, Wolfe was committed to a presentation of a one-man "vision of life." Society was significant only as this one man saw it. Wolfe's vision came from a sincere evaluation of the facts of life as he had gathered them, and the resulting attitude he took toward them. Wolfe knew what he was doing and thus he called himself "artist," for in his creation he was providing an aesthetic experience—that which led from creation to discovery and finally to form. In his quest for experience for the purpose of art, Wolfe was in the company of Melville, Whitman, and Mark Twain.

135

It was as artist, then, that Wolfe recorded the reality of the world from the point of view of the individual. He was not constrained to attain the high mountaintops of abstract truth. To view the absolute, as Plato and Jesus and Shakespeare saw it, required journeying to the barrens for reflection. The wilderness was not for Wolfe. He was concerned with America and with its people around him, with the tragic waste and the poetic fulfillment. Out of the treasure house of his abounding life came the wherewithal for his assignment as artist. The task of the artist is, Miller wrote in *Tropic of Cancer,* "to overthrow existing values, to make of the chaos about him an order which is his own, to sow strife and ferment so that by the emotional release those who are dead may be restored to life."

It was the "chaos about him" which disturbed Wolfe. If he took to heart the familiar Emerson statement with which he was certainly familiar, "Only so much do I know, as I have lived," he needed to look no further for a state of chaos on which to impose an order of his own. Though Wolfe formulated his literary principles later, the immense *romans à clef,* with an autobiographical hero at their center, had their beginning in aesthetic experience. They were neither diaries of self-confession, not the sprawling personal histories of a frenzied scatterbrain; nor, indeed, were they the definitive story of Thomas Wolfe. There were similarities between Gant and Wolfe and between people the novelist knew and the characters he put into his books, but Wolfe insisted on the literary subtlety of difference. To frequent charges, he had a reply:

> I don't "write about" people: I create living characters of my own—a whole universe of my own creation. And any character that I create is so unmistakably my own that anyone familiar with my work would know instantly it was my own, even if it had no title and no name.

This is a fair defense of style and method, if any is required. Even so, it took Wolfe some time to find out that the factual details were unnecessary. He had to learn, he said, that though one may write about a horse thief, he did not need to give his address and telephone number.

For the writing of *romans à clef,* Wolfe had many honorable predecessors, including Tolstoi and Proust and Joyce, to say nothing of Melville and Mark Twain in America. As a matter of fact, *Look Homeward, Angel* is no closer to undisguised actuality than *Redburn* or *Life on the Mississippi.* Yet the conversion of experience into impersonal terms, Tolstoi's artistic forte, and Melville's often, was never really possible for Wolfe. Perhaps he took the harder, if less artistic, way: he accepted the role of transforming his very life into a sensuous fiction which would distill the essence of a country from the experiences and vision of one man. If this was hopeless aspiration, he was no less willing to try to see whether it could be done.

As we know, one of the ways he went about his task was to shift to lyricism whenever straight exposition was inadequate to express the truth of a situation or emotion. This poetic quality not only saturates the language but also governs the rhythm of sentences and paragraphs and even chapters. Beyond style, Wolfe employed it to translate the exhilaration of a youth who, in Emerson's words about such a one, "woke in the morning with an appetite that could eat the solar system like a cake." In Wolfe and his heroes was the endearing innocence of an inquisitive and famished child, a newborn child looking out upon the fresh wonders of the earth with sublime perception.

This innocence and exuberance demanded a poetry that, when it lost its lyric overtones, exposed itself as rhetoric. Wolfe could work himself up to a frenzy of words which matched the high-powered oratorical style of nineteenth-century American speechmakers. In these declamatory passages, he harked back to the guise of legislative debaters, to the rapid verbal flow of Whitman and Melville. When W. O. Gant spouts his long tirades, he is being nothing so much as grandchild to that raving madman Ahab. Similarly, Eugene and George can be no less incensed at the damnation inflicted upon their spirits, and when they are in their agonies they lash forth with words rather than swords. There is a mighty, primitive poetry in these passages. Nothing is small; for in such moments these small-town heroes assume the dimensions of tortured ancient warriors whipping the world for its insensibility. Even when Wolfe allowed his exaggerations to slip into caricature, he was merely letting his reader understand the basically comic nature of man's pretentiousness.

Rhetoric and poetry, natural endowments of a Southerner like Wolfe, are among the few characteristics which tie him to Southern writing. His novels concern no problems which can be said to be typically Southern. Yet his roots, which were strongly planted in his native culture, stretched down more deeply as the years passed. Whenever his purposes suited, he exploited his folk heritage, and the bigness of his exaggerated characters and the rambunctiousness of their rhetoric are based in the tall-tales tradition of the Southern frontier. Creations like W. O. Gant, bigger than life, have about them such an epic grandeur that they seem concocted of lore and legend and myth. In fact, Herbert J. Muller discusses Wolfe as "myth-maker"—as one who, in contemporary parlance, provides within his narrative the unchanging patterns of life; and the controlling image of Wolfe's patterns, he discovered, was "the great national myth, the American dream." The patterns of mythmakers are implicit in the traditions and legends of the kind of folk culture which was Wolfe's because of his birth. Muller concludes that, while Wolfe was certainly no Homer, "his life work was perhaps as close as we can expect to come to an American epic."

When a man with Wolfe's memory and energy begins to set down his life and heritage with an announced American-wide breadth, something unusual is bound to happen. At hand was an abundance of material so unlimited that Wolfe, again and again, cried out his need for control. He admitted that condensation and brevity were difficult for him and that his greatest fear was that he could not keep mastery of himself and his goods. It was surely a feat of strength that his superabundance was held in check as well as it was. The main thing is that Wolfe understood his problem, and yet he also understood what he had to do. When Fitzgerald wrote him that, though his talent was "unmatchable in this or any other country," he ought to strive like Flaubert to write "the novel of selected incidents," Wolfe's good-humored reply was a defense of the putter-inners:

There are no novels of unselected incidents . . . Just remember that although "Madame Bovary" in your opinion may be a great book, "Tristram Shandy" *is* indubitably a great book, and that it is great for quite different reasons. It is great because it *boils* and *pours*—for the *unselected* quality of its selection. You say that the great writer like Flaubert has consciously left out the stuff that Bill or Joe will come along presently and put in. Well, don't forget, Scott, that a great writer is not only a leaver-outer but also a putter-inner, and that Shakespeare and Cervantes and Dostoievsky were great putter-inners—greater putter-inners, in fact, than taker-outers—and will be remembered for what they put in—remembered, I venture to say, as long as Monsieur Flaubert will be remembered for what he left out.

Putter-inners are concerned with the form of life itself, which rarely works itself out in plot or selected incidents. In no sense was Wolfe a plot-mechanic. He, like Melville, felt he had no need to invent plots or characters. His artistic creations welled from living people and incidents. Literature, viewed in this way, was not a matter of one thing being good and another thing being bad. W. O. Gant was neither hero nor villain; Eliza could be both mercenary and indulgent. Wolfe never failed to show compassion for all of his characters, even for the esthetes and phonies whom he despised. Thus his novels have the stuff of life in them—a fact recognized by those

who abhorred his failure to write "the novel of selected incidents." Aswell noted that his characters had a habit of going
about their lives in an everyday sort of way, of moving from
book to book, and often of simply "dropping out of sight and
being forgotten."

The individual segments of his "one book" have their own
special narratives, of course; their unifying force owes nothing to artificial form but, as is true of the seemingly discon-
nected parts of Whitman's *Leaves of Grass,* rather to the powerful personality of their author. The books taken together
may be considered the story of the spiritual development in the
life of a young man, his education in the world, and his eventual attainment of belief.

In spite of his achievements, Wolfe was not, being human,
by any means the perfect writer. During his life and since his
death, his deviations from the accepted, especially his unortho-
dox form and lavish style, have been called to the bar over
and over again; and a certain circle of critics has denounced
him so vehemently that it would seem that his books could not
survive. When the novels continued to attract attention, these
critics resorted to ignoring Wolfe entirely. Many full-length
criticisms of American writing published in the 1950's did not
mention him at all.

The denunciations have been florid: "grandiose rubbish,"
said W. H. Auden; "disorganized gusto," echoed Louis Unter-
meyer. "He seemed sad, really, like Carnera," wrote Ernest
Hemingway in *Green Hills of Africa.* Even William Faulkner,
who placed Wolfe at the top of his contemporaries, wrote of
him as "the best failure" and explained the epithet by calling
attention to Wolfe's willingness, he said, "to throw away style,
coherence, all the rules of preciseness, [in order] to try to put
all the experience of the human heart on the head of a pin, as
it were." Most of the critical strictures dealt with Wolfe's
flouting a lack of discipline, with his disregard of literary rules,
and with a confusion of art and autobiography.

There have always been, or course, defenders who were quick

to denounce the detractors and to point out wherein they were misled. But since neither side ever convinced the other, the contest has never abated, not does it seem likely that it will, till Time herself provides mediation.

The obstreperous name-calling aside, a principal concern remains as to whether Wolfe actually wrote novels. That he did not do so was the contention of those who, beginning in the 1930's, began to preach a neo-orthodoxy in literature. These critics repudiated the subjective, asked that a writer withdraw himself from his fiction, and demanded that he emphasize form. The careful structure of a work on certain principles, generally those laid down by Henry James, was called for. In a world where lawlessness was rampant, literature was to be corseted by predigested labels and preconceived regulations. To be recognized as an artist by those arbiters of what was what in literature, one had to conform.

Wolfe, needless to say, was no conformist. He groaned at what critics had to say, he would have pleased them if he could and from time to time he tried to do so, but at every attempt he jumped the fence before he could rope himself or be roped. Perhaps he recognized the mediocre, bloodless productions which proceeded from capitulation to formulae.

At any rate Wolfe wished to make his book fit life, not to make life fit his book. He was anti-intellectual in that he was not ashamed to be emotionally aroused, not ashamed to *feel* as well as to think. And finally he was not so involved with structure that he forgot moral values and living character.

Wolfe novels, it can be said, do not deviate so much from the novel as practiced and defined in Western literature of the last several hundred years, as they deviate from the prescriptions set up by the New Conservatives, who decried experiments in form and, more seriously, censured optimism and democracy. The disapprobation of the New Conservatives—composed of New Humanists, Neo-Thomists, Southern Agrarians, New Critics, and others—killed off most of the dissenters, but not Wolfe, who was hardy enough to survive the onslaught.

In *You Can't Go Home Again,* Lloyd McHarg admonished George Webber to listen to none of the critics who scolded him for not writing differently, but to go on doing what he had to do. Wolfe, in real life, was not quite able to take this advice, but he came as near to it as he could. If he was frequently extravagant and diffuse and if he often erred in defining his own rules, at least he had the consolation of knowing that he was always himself.

The fact remains that Wolfe has always been constantly read. He has not been resurrected like Fitzgerald, nor was he revived during his own lifetime like Faulkner, nor like Hemingway has he had much of his work handed over to the academicians. The several decades following an author's death constitute his most perilous probation, for during that time he drops from the contemporary scene and some decision is made about his lasting qualities. We have observed Wolfe's endurance despite strong critical opposition.

A brief look at where Wolfe stands on the ladder of American literature will indicate some of the reasons why this has been so. The odd thing is that Wolfe never assessed his position in terms of American writing. Whenever he tried to place himself, he thought of English writers and aspired to the company of Chaucer, Donne, Defoe, Sterne, Fielding, Smollett, Coleridge, and Dickens. Or he placed himself among those great putter-inners. Perhaps this was natural, for his schooling in literature was in the British and continental writers. On university campuses before 1925 American authors were seldom studied with the seriousness given Europeans. At any rate, Muller concedes that Wolfe belongs to the classic tradition with Homer and Shakespeare and all the others who built a literature on the folklore and resources of a national heritage.

It is odd, too, that though Wolfe's most declared admiration among his contemporaries was for James Joyce, a skilled artisan, he was apparently uninfluenced by the Irishman's craftsmanship. Wolfe's indebtedness to Joyce lay elsewhere.

Wolfe's reputation, obviously, must be measured in American terms. It may be as simple as that he was a big man physically, like Melville and Dreiser, in a big country and that he had, like them, to write big American novels. It may be that his seeming intemperance and excess flowed from an urge, again like Melville's, to put a heart into America. He had humor, like Mark Twain and Sinclair Lewis, but unlike them, there was no real malice in it. It may be that in writing the new novel of sensibility, he saw, like Faulkner and Henry Miller (to paraphrase Alfred Kazin), the unhappiness of his relations with America and in gargantuan proportions made epics out of his conflict. It may be that Wolfe will be remembered primarily as a voice of his decade, detailing the greed and bacchanalia which preceded the collapse of a country before it could find itself.

In the final analysis, however, Wolfe's success or failure rests on his adventure with the American Dream, as this Dream was developed from the time of Jefferson on through Emerson and Whitman up to the first quarter of the twentieth century. The Dream encompassed the hopes of young men everywhere for democracy and liberty and equality and individuality. It was an ideal and a promise. Wolfe was an American writer, not only because his problems were those of an American within America, but because his youth demanded fulfillment in a land where individual fulfillment was possible. In this Dream, it was Whitman who was his nearest spirit. Each of them spoke poetically out of his loneliness for all the young artists—and every young man is an artist to himself—across the sweep and breadth of the great land.

Before he completed his investigation into the nature of permanent acceptance in America, Wolfe had won within himself the struggle which is the essence of all human drama. With courage and honor, he had discovered through experience that his lot was common to that of all men. Out of his life and out of this discovery came the books.

SELECTED BIBLIOGRAPHY

NOTE: Works available in paperbound editions are so indicated at the conclusion of the entry.

WOLFE'S CHIEF WORKS

Look Homeward, Angel. New York: Scribner, 1929. (Paperbound)
Of Time and the River. New York: Scribner, 1935.
The Web and the Rock. New York: Harper, 1939. (Paperbound)
You Can't Go Home Again. New York: Harper, 1940. (Paperbound)

SHORT WORKS

From Death to Morning. New York: Scribner, 1935.
The Story of a Novel. New York: Scribner, 1936.
A Note on Experts: Dexter Vespasian Joyner. New York: House of Books, 1939.
The Hills Beyond. New York: Harper, 1941. [With a valuable "Note" by Edward C. Aswell.] (Paperbound)
"The Years of Wandering in many lands and cities." New York: Charles S. Boesen, 1949. [With an unsigned foreword by George R. Preston, Jr., reproduces six holograph pages written by Wolfe during the last months of his life.]
A Western Journal. Pittsburgh: University of Pittsburgh Press, 1951. [Carefully reproduced from Wolfe's notebooks.]

PLAYS

Mannerhouse. New York: Harper, 1948.
Welcome to Our City, abridged. *Esquire* (October, 1957). [Two of his undergraduate one-act plays, "The Return of Buck Gavin" and "The Third Night," appeared in *Carolina Folk-Plays,* ed. Frederick H. Koch, New York: Holt, 1941.]

COLLECTED SELECTIONS

The Face of a Nation. New York: Scribner, 1939. [Poetic passages selected by John Hall Wheelock.]
A Stone, a Leaf, a Door. New York: Scribner, 1946. [Rearranged into verse by John S. Barnes.]
The Portable Thomas Wolfe, ed. Maxwell Geismar. New York: Viking, 1946.

LETTERS

Thomas Wolfe's Letters to His Mother, ed. John Skally Terry. New York: Scribner, 1943.
The Correspondence of Thomas Wolfe and Homer Andrew Watt, eds. Oscar Cargill and Thomas Clark Pollock. New York: New York University Press, 1954.

Thomas Wolfe

The Letters of Thomas Wolfe, ed. Elizabeth Nowell. New York: Scribner, 1956.
[Other letters include those to Mrs. Roberts, reprinted in the *Atlantic Monthly* (December, 1946; January, February, 1947). Only a few of his letters to Mrs. Bernstein have been published. Significant letters to Wolfe appear in *Editor to Author: The Letters of Maxwell E. Perkins* (New York: Scribner, 1950) (Paperbound) and *Letters of Sherwood Anderson* (Boston: Little, Brown, 1953).]

BIBLIOGRAPHY

Full-Length

Johnson, Elmer D. *Of Time and Thomas Wolfe: a Bibliography with a Character Index of His Works.* New York: Scarecrow Press, 1959. [For the most part without annotations.]
Preston, George R., Jr. *Thomas Wolfe: a Bibliography.* New York: Charles S. Boesen, 1943. [Particularly helpful because of its annotations of and excerpts from the various entries.]

Short Works

Holman, Hugh C. "Thomas Wolfe: a Bibliographical Study," *Texas Studies in Literature and Language* (Autumn, 1959).
Leary, Lewis. *Articles on American Literature, 1900–1950.* Durham: Duke University Press, 1954.
Spiller, Robert E., et al. *Literary History of the United States,* Vol. III, *Bibliography.* New York: Macmillan, 1948. *Supplement,* ed. Richard M. Ludwig. New York: Macmillan, 1959.
[Current additions are found in the annual bibliography of *Publications of the Modern Language Association,* the quarterly *American Literature,* and the monthly *Abstracts of English Studies.*]

BIOGRAPHY

Full-Length

Nowell, Elizabeth. *Thomas Wolfe.* Garden City: Doubleday, 1960.

Specialized Essays

Adams, Agatha Boyd. *Thomas Wolfe: Carolina Student.* Chapel Hill: University of North Carolina Library, 1950. [Wolfe's undergraduate years at the University of North Carolina.]
Armstrong, Anne W. "As I Saw Thomas Wolfe," *Arizona Quarterly* (Spring, 1946).
Blythe, LeGette. "The Thomas Wolfe I Knew," *Saturday Review* (August 25, 1945).
Daniels, Jonathan. *Tar Heels: A Portrait of North Carolina.* New York: Dodd, Mead, 1941.
Dodd, Martha. *Through Embassy Eyes.* New York: Harcourt, Brace, 1939.
Kennedy, Richard S. "Thomas Wolfe at Harvard, 1920–1923," *Harvard Library Bulletin* (Spring, Autumn, 1950).
Ledig-Rowohlt, Heinrich M. "Thomas Wolfe in Berlin," *American Scholar* (Spring, 1953).
Norwood, Hayden. *The Marble Man's Wife: Thomas Wolfe's Mother.* New York: Scribner, 1947. [A "conversational biography."]

146

Pollock, Thomas Clark, and Cargill, Oscar. *Thomas Wolfe at Washington Square*. New York: New York University Press, 1954. [His teaching career at New York University.]

Walser, Richard (ed.). *The Enigma of Thomas Wolfe: Biographical and Critical Selections*. Cambridge: Harvard University Press, 1953. [Includes eight biographical and seventeen critical essays.]

[Nine articles on Wolfe and his family, generally overlooked, were written by Frank A. Dickson and appeared in the *Independent* of Anderson, South Carolina (July 10, 15, 24, 29, August 7, 14, 19, 26, September 2, 1948).]

CRITICAL AND INTERPRETATIVE STUDIES

Full-Length

Johnson, Pamela Hansford. *Hungry Gulliver, an English Critical Appraisal*. New York: Scribner, 1948. [Emphasizes the peculiarly American quality of Wolfe's fiction.]

Muller, Herbert J. *Thomas Wolfe*. Norfolk, Conn.: New Directions, 1947. [Attempts to balance two extremes of criticism but centers on the author's contributions as Mythmaker.]

Rubin, Louis D., Jr. *Thomas Wolfe: the Weather of His Youth*. Baton Rouge: Louisiana State University Press, 1955. [Portrays Wolfe as essentially the product of his heredity and environment.]

Watkins, Floyd C. *Thomas Wolfe's Characters: Portraits from Life*. Norman: University of Oklahoma Press, 1957. [Traces the sources of Wolfe's semiautobiographical fiction.]

Brief Analyses

Brodin, Pierre. *Thomas Wolfe*. Asheville: Stephens Press, 1949.

Heath, John R. *The Strange Case of Thomas Wolfe*. Chicago: Chicago Literary Club, 1949.

Holman, C. Hugh. *Thomas Wolfe*. Minneapolis: University of Minnesota Press, 1960.

Foreign Doctoral Papers

Delakas, Daniel L. *Thomas Wolfe, la France, et les Romanciers Français*. Paris: Jouve, 1950.

Pfister, Karin. *Zeit und Wirklichkeit bei Thomas Wolfe*. Heidelberg: Carl Winter, 1954.

Reeves, George M., Jr. *Thomas Wolfe et l'Europe*. Paris: Jouve, 1955. [Scores of unpublished American theses and dissertations on Wolfe are listed in the Johnson bibliography.]

Wolfe in Perspective

Beach, Joseph Warren. *American Fiction, 1920–1940*. New York: Macmillan, 1941.

Boynton, Percy H. *America in Contemporary Fiction*. Chicago: University of Chicago Press, 1940.

Geismar, Maxwell. *Writers in Crisis: The American Novel Between Two Wars*. Boston: Houghton Mifflin, 1942.

Gelfant, Blanche Housman. *The American City Novel*. Norman: University of Oklahoma Press, 1954.

Gurko, Leo. *The Angry Decade*. New York: Dodd, Mead, 1947.

Thomas Wolfe

Hoffman, Frederick J. *The Modern Novel in America, 1900–1950.* Chicago: H. Regnery Co., 1951. (Paperbound)

Hicks, Granville (ed.). *The Living Novel.* New York: Macmillan, 1957.

Kazin, Alfred. *On Native Grounds: An Interpretation of Modern American Prose Literature.* New York: Reynal & Hitchcock, 1942. (Paperbound)

Snell, George. *The Shapers of American Fiction, 1798–1947.* New York: E. P. Dutton, 1947.

Spiller, Robert E. *The Cycle of American Literature.* New York: Macmillan, 1955. (Paperbound)

Stovall, Floyd. *American Idealism.* Norman: University of Oklahoma Press, 1943.

Critical Articles

Albrecht, W. P. "The Titles of *Look Homeward, Angel,*" *Modern Language Quarterly* (March, 1950).

——, "Time as Unity in Thomas Wolfe," *New Mexico Quarterly Review* (Autumn, 1949).

Budd, Louis J. "The Grotesques of Anderson and Wolfe," *Modern Fiction Studies* (Winter, 1959–60).

Coughlan, Robert. "Tom Wolfe's Surge to Greatness," *Life* (September 17, 1956); "Grand Vision, A Final Tragedy," *Life* (September 24, 1956).

Cowley, Malcolm. "Thomas Wolfe," *Atlantic Monthly* (November, 1957).

Curley, Thomas F. "Thomas Wolfe: Novelist of the Normal," *Commonweal* (November 23, 1956).

Delakas, Daniel L. "Thomas Wolfe and Anatole France," *Comparative Literature* (Winter, 1957).

Foster, Ruel E. "Fabulous Tom Wolfe," *University of Kansas City Review* (Summer, 1957).

Golden, Harry. "Thomas Wolfe," *Carolina Israelite* (September–October, 1956).

Halperin, Irving. "Wolfe's *Of Time and the River,*" *Explicator* (November, 1959).

Holman, C. Hugh. "The Loneliness at the Core," *New Republic* (October 10, 1955).

McElderry, B. R. "The Durable Humor of *Look Homeward, Angel,*" *Arizona Quarterly* (Summer, 1955).

Stevens, Virginia. "Thomas Wolfe's America," *Mainstream* (January, 1958).

Watkins, Floyd C. "Thomas Wolfe's High Sinfulness of Poetry," *Modern Fiction Studies* (December, 1956).

Williams, Cecil B. "Thomas Wolfe Fifteen Years After," *South Atlantic Quarterly* (October, 1955).

Three collections of Wolfe materials far surpass all others in American libraries. The Houghton Library at Harvard preserves intact the vast William B. Wisdom collection of Wolfe's manuscripts along with his personal books and clippings. The University of North Carolina Library is strong on materials about Wolfe, but special enrichment has come from donations of family documents and mementoes, in addition to the extensive manuscript materials gathered by John S. Terry in preparation for a never-written biography. The most nearly complete file of printed matter on Wolfe, however, is in the Pack Memorial Public Library in Asheville, North Carolina.

INDEX

Note: Characters and other fictional subjects from Wolfe's works are entered in small capital letters.

Index

Harcourt, Brace, 37
Harpers, 50, 92, 105, 117
Harvard University, 10, 25–28 *passim,*
   73–79 *passim,* 89, 119, 134
HATCHER, PROFESSOR, 25, 77, 78
Hemingway, Ernest, 38, 132, 135, 140,
   142
"HOME TO OUR MOUNTAINS," 107, 110
Hotel Albert, New York, 30
Hotel Chelsea, New York, 49, 50
HOTEL LEOPOLD, 31, 82
Hotel Saint George, Brooklyn, 112
Houghton Library, Harvard, 119
Howard, Sidney, 25

JACK, ESTHER, 34, 92–110 *passim*
JACK, FREDERICK, 108
JAMES, LAURA, 21, 57
JAMES RODNEY & CO., 107
Jews, 5, 34, 80, 82, 90, 99, 102, 109,
   115
Johns Hopkins Hospital, 13, 27, 51
JOHNSON, DOCTOR, 120, 121
Johnson, Gerald, 50
Johnson, Pamela Hansford, 78
JONES, ABE, 80
Journey Down, The, by Aline Bern-
   stein, 104
Joyce, James, 9, 35, 67–85 *passim,* 127,
   137, 142
JOYNER, AUNT MAW, 15, 95, 107
JOYNER FAMILY, 92, 94, 96, 97
JOYNER, LAFAYETTE, 130
JOYNER, ROBERT, 129
JOYNER, RUFUS, 129
JOYNER, THEODORE, 129
JOYNER, WILLIAM "BEAR," 129
JOYNER, ZACHARIAH, 129

KATAMOTO, MR., 107
Kazin, Alfred, 7, 94, 112, 135, 143
Kittredge, George Lyman, 28
Koch, Frederick H., 22, 23, 24, 26

Langfeld, Herbert Sidney, 28
Langner, Lawrence, 31
LEONARD, JOHN DORSEY, 18–19, 57
LEONARD, MARGARET, 19, 57
Lewis, Sinclair, 9, 41, 70, 75, 113, 114,
   134, 143
LIBYA HILL, 92–110 *passim,* 129
LOGAN, PIGGY, 109
London, 6, 35, 41, 113, 114, 123
Lowes, John Livingston, 25, 27, 28

MCHARG, LLOYD, 41, 113, 114, 142
McIlwain, Charles Howard, 28
MALONE, SEAMUS, 37, 100
Melville, Herman, 64, 135–143 *passim*
Mencken, H. L., 132
Miller, Henry, 9, 135, 136, 143
Milton, John, 9, 64, 65
Miss Condon, by Aline Bernstein, 104
Mitchell, Skinner, 25
Muller, Herbert J., 139, 142

Munich, 37, 101, 103, 107, 124
Murray, John Tucker, 28

Negroes, 5, 29, 58, 120, 122
New York University, 31, 34
North Carolina, 3, 14, 21, 39–53 *pas-
   sim,* 126, 129
North State Fitting School, 19, 22
Nowell, Elizabeth, 49, 105, 106, 132

OLD CATAWBA, 5, 54, 67, 75, 85, 94, 95,
   124, 130
"Old Kentucky Home, The," 18, 21, 49
O'Neill, Eugene, 25, 100, 122
Orange Street School, 16, 18

Paris, 32, 40, 44, 84–87 *passim,* 123
Pater, Walter, 26
Paul, Clara, 21, 22
Pennsylvania, 14, 54, 79, 94, 130
PENTLAND FAMILY, 129
PENTLAND, JOHN, 127
PENTLAND, UNCLE BASCOM, 78, 127
Perkins, Maxwell, 37–52 *passim,* 73,
   74, 123, 131
PIERCE, JOEL, 32, 82
PINE ROCK COLLEGE, 97
PROSSER, DICK, 95
Proust, Marcel, 12, 63, 78, 87, 137
PULPIT HILL, 57, 87, 97
PURVIS, DAISY, 113

Raisbeck, Kenneth, 28, 32, 33
Raleigh, N.C., 14, 20, 47
RAMSAY, EUGENE, 122
RAMSAY, GENERAL, 122
RANDOLPH, JIM, 97, 98
RAWNG AND WRIGHT, 100
Roberts, J. M., 18
Roberts, Margaret, 10, 19, 63
Rubin, Louis D., 101
RUTLEDGE, 120

Saint Louis Exposition, 2, 16, 56, 126
SCHOOL OF UTILITY CULTURES, 99, 111
Scribners, 37–47 *passim,* 107, 123
SCUDDER, LULU, 37, 101, 107
Shakespeare, 8, 19, 28, 58, 136, 139
SHEPPERTON, RANDY, 95, 108, 110
SIMPSON FAMILY, 79
STARWICK, FRANCIS, 28, 78, 79, 84, 85
Steinbeck, John, 135
Sterne, Laurence, 139, 142
Stevens, Virginia, 74
"Stone, a leaf, a door, A," symbol, 66
Swinnerton, Frank, 41

Terry, John S., 32, 44, 46
Theatre Guild, 30, 122
Three Blue Suits, by Aline Bernstein,
   104
Twain, Mark, 49, 135, 137, 143

University of North Carolina, 20–24

150

Index